WILLIAM H. MOBLEY
Texas A & M University

Employee Turnover: Causes, Consequences, and Control

ADDISON-WESLEY PUBLISHING COMPANY

*Reading, Massachusetts · Menlo Park, California
London · Amsterdam · Don Mills, Ontario · Sydney*

THE ADDISON-WESLEY SERIES ON MANAGING HUMAN RESOURCES

Series Editor: John P. Wanous, Michigan State University

Fairness in Selecting Employees
Richard D. Arvey, University of Houston

Organizational Entry: Recruitment, Selection, and Socialization of Newcomers
John P. Wanous, Michigan State University

Increasing Productivity through Performance Appraisal
Gary P. Latham, University of Washington, and Kenneth N. Wexley,
Michigan State University

Managing Conflict at Organizational Interfaces
David Brown, Brown University

Employee Turnover: Causes, Consequences and Control
William H. Mobley, Texas A & M University

Managing Careers
Manuel London, AT&T and Stephen A. Stumpf,
N.Y. University

Library of Congress Cataloging in Publication Data

Mobley, William H.
    Employee turnover, causes, consequences, and control.

    (Managing human resources)
    Bibliography: p.
    Includes indexes.
    1. Labor turnover. 2. Personnel management.
I. Title. II. Series.
HF5549.5.T8M6   658.3'14   81-20485
ISBN 0-201-04673-3   AACR2

ISBN 0-201-04673-3
ABCDEFGHIJ-AL-898765432

Series Foreword

Widespread attention given to the effective management of human resources came of age in the 1970s. As we enter the 1980s, the importance placed on it continues to grow. Personnel departments, which used to be little more than the keepers of employee files, are now moving to the forefront in corporate visibility.

The difficulties encountered in effective human resource management are without parallel. Surveys of managers and top level executives consistently show "human problems" at the top of most lists. The influx of the behavioral sciences into business school programs is further testimony to the active concern now placed on human resources as a crucial element in organizational effectiveness.

The primary objective of this Addison-Wesley series is to articulate new solutions to chronic human resource problems; for example, the selection and entry of newcomers, performance appraisal, leadership, conflict management and career management. The aim is to communicate with a variety of audiences, including present managers, students as future managers, and fellow professionals in business, government, and academia.

John P. Wanous
Series Editor

To Robert S. Ramsay

Mentor, Colleague, and Friend

Preface

This book is designed to be a managerial and personnel research-oriented treatment of employee turnover. The book should be of interest to students of human resource management, organizational behavior, and industrial-personnel psychology, and to professional personnel managers, personnel researchers, and other managers. Although the book is managerially oriented, we focus on the perspective of the individual employee as well. Thus the book should also be of value to students and managers as they contemplate their individual careers. Further, some of the concepts, extensive references, and emphasis on gaps in understanding should be of value to the researcher with a theoretical interest in turnover.

Employee turnover is important to organizations, individuals, and society. From the organizational perspective, employee turnover can represent a significant cost in terms of lost recruiting, training, socialization investments, disruption and replacement costs, and a variety of indirect costs. Conversely, employee turnover can have positive organizational benefits via, for example, displacement of poor performers, creation of promotion opportunities, and infusion of new people with new ideas.

From the individual perspective, turnover can have potentially positive and/or negative consequences. For example, the decision to quit a job can be positively associated with the pursuit of an individual's career objectives or with the movement away from a stressful situation. Alternatively, turnover can have negative implications for the individual. For example, the individual may lose nonvested benefits, may disrupt the family's social support system, and can be subject to the "grass looks greener" phenomenon only to experience later disillusionment. Further, turnover can have positive and/or negative implications for the individuals who remain with the organization.

Finally, from the societal perspective, turnover again can be seen to have potentially positive and/or negative consequences. Turnover is associated with mobility and migration to new industries and organizations—necessary for economic development. Conversely, excessive turnover could serve to depress productivity growth and orderly development.

Given the significance of turnover from these three perspectives, it is important for the manager and prospective manager to be able to analyze, understand, and effectively manage employee turnover. This book is devoted to these ends.

The book is divided into four major components dealing with: (1) causes and correlates of employee turnover; (2) conceptual models; (3) consequences of turnover; and (4) analysis and control of turnover. The Appendix presents a stimulating treatment of force-loss cost analysis by H.W. Gustafson, Manager of Human Performance Systems at AT&T. Throughout the book, both the positive and negative individual and organizational implications of turnover are discussed. Although societal implications receive some attention, detailed discussion of societal issues is beyond the scope of this book.

The recent literature on employee turnover, organizational behavior, organizational entry, socialization, personnel management, human resource accounting, and personnel information systems are extensively utilized. Materials and examples from a variety of organizational settings including manufacturing, hospitals, the military, and banking are integrated in the text. Material from several foreign settings is utilized in recognition of the increased multinationalization of business and the fact that turnover is not a western phenomenon.

We appreciate the many authors and researchers who have contributed to the body of knowledge on employee turnover, in particular March and Simon (1958), Vroom (1964), Porter and Steers (1973), Locke (1976), and Price (1977). We also thank: the organizations who provided materials used to demonstrate various turnover analysis and control methods; H.W. Gustafson for his authorship of the Appendix; the Office of Naval Research for funding a significant portion of the author's earlier research on turnover; and to colleagues H.P. Dachler, H.H. Hand, S.O. Horner, B. M. Meglino, and S. A. Youngblood with whom I had the privilege of collaborating on earlier turnover research. Finally, a special word of thanks to John P. Wanous, editor of this series, to Janis Jackson Hill, Addison-Wesley editor; and to Edward E. Lawler III, of the University of Southern California, Barry Baysinger of Texas A & M University, and Stanley O. Horner of Texas Instruments for their cogent reviews of earlier drafts.

This book is dedicated to Dr. Robert S. Ramsay of PPG Industries. Bob was instrumental in stimulating my interest in industrial psychology and for many years has been a valued role model, colleague, and friend.

College Station, Texas   W.H.M.
January, 1982

Contents

Employee Turnover: An Overview

1

INTRODUCTION

Employee turnover — people leaving organizations — is a major organizational phenomenon. In recognition of this fact, turnover is included in many definitions of "organizational effectiveness" (Steers, 1977). It would, however, be simplistic to view turnover from only a negative perspective since there are occasions when turnover has positive organizational implications (Staw, 1980). It would be further simplistic to view turnover from only the organization's perspective. Turnover is an important behavior from individual and societal perspectives as well (Dalton and Todor, 1979). Additionally, it is important to consider the consequences of turnover on the individuals who remain — a frequently overlooked perspective (Mowday, 1981; Steers and Mowday, 1981).

This book is devoted to those interested in better understanding and managing employee turnover. Understanding and effectively managing employee turnover requires:

1. Integrating individual, organizational, and environmental perspectives;

2. Recognizing both the positive and the negative potential consequences of turnover;

3. Basing strategies for dealing with turnover on economic and cost data, employee perception, attitudinal and behavioral data, and individual and organizational evaluative data;

4. Recognizing that turnover, with its multiple causes and consequences, is an ongoing *process,* not a static event;

5. Finally, adopting a *proactive* rather than reactive posture.

This introductory chapter illustrates some of the implications of turnover for individuals, organizations, and society. In addition, we will present documentation relevant to the scope of the phenomenon and discuss the definition of turnover. Finally, we will present a managerial perspective for understanding, analyzing, and controlling turnover and preview the subsequent chapters.

SOME ILLUSTRATIVE CASES

A. After only six months in a management-training program, Sara Fripp was so disillusioned with her job that she quit. Sara's employer had to find a replacement, and they lost the recruiting, moving, and training costs invested in her. Sara now had to start a new job search and was questioning her own competence.

> *Comment:* Sara is one of many who leave their first job after only a short period of time. Understanding this early attrition is important if organizations are to minimize its associated costs and disruptiveness and assist individuals in making better job and career decisions.

B. Dr. Nathanial Evans joined the research staff of Century Electronics primarily because of the reputation of the researchers he would be working with. Within two years, three of them had left the company, and their replacements were not providing the stimulation he needed and desired. Dr. Evans felt isolated, betrayed, and unproductive.

> *Comment:* Dr. Evans's plight illustrates the fact that turnover can have an important impact, in this case negative, on individuals who remain. There are also situations where turnover would have a positive influence on those who remain — for example, when those who leave are incompetent or disruptive.

C. John McVail has just responded to an inquiry from Executive Search, Inc. Although he has been with his employer for 12 years, has received only the highest performance and potential ratings, and has received good pay increases, he sees no chance for promotion because there is no turnover among the deadwood on his career path.

> *Comment:* This case illustrates how lack of turnover and/or opportunity for upward mobility can lead to turnover among lower-level competent employees. Diagnosing and dealing with this issue are important management functions.

D. Joan Cordova, with a college degree in French, was working for a steel company as an "administrative assistant." She was bored with her job, frequently absent while she looked for alternative jobs, and increasingly irritable at work. After extensive search she found a job in the international division of a major bank; 24 months later she became an officer and was transferred to the Paris branch.

> *Comment:* Joan was underutilized in her former position and was exhibiting negative symptoms from both individual and organizational perspectives. Her departure led to a rewarding career path consistent with her abilities and aspirations. The outcome was positive for Joan and her new employer — and probably for her former employer as well.

E. After hearing a presentation on human resources accounting at the American Management Association, Rob Howard, vice-president of manufacturing for a synthetic fiber company, established a study team from personnel, accounting, and manufacturing. The team was instructed to conduct a cost-benefit analysis of the production employee turnover problem and alternative strategies for dealing with the problem. Howard was astonished to learn that a *conservative* estimate of annual turnover cost in only one of his plants was $450,000.

> *Comment:* To effectively manage turnover, one needs analyses dealing with both the costs and the consequences of turnover, and cost-benefits of counter-attrition strategies. Advances in human resource accounting (see Appendix A)

can help provide a framework for such analyses. Managers like Ron Howard need good data if they are to manage turnover effectively.

F. J.C. Derrick, the manager of a Southern shirt factory, placed an urgent call to his New York headquarters. He had 30 sewing machines sitting idle because his employees were quitting and going to a new tire plant on the other side of town. Derrick was already fighting a slim profit margin, foreign competition, and a tight labor market. What was to be done?

Comment: The organizational implications of turnover can extend beyond direct turnover and replacement costs — in this case, idle machines and major loss of productivity. Given a tight labor market and a profit margin precluding direct wage competition, the organization must find alternative strategies for recruiting and retaining employees. The situation is not hopeless.

G. Dorchester County Bank, a small rural bank, instituted a sound merit compensation system in 1978. After three years under this system several long-time poor performers, dissatisfied with their pay increases, quit the bank. Through aggressive recruiting, careful selection, and no increase in the salary budget, the bank hired two experienced replacements. One provided valuable new knowledge on electronic banking; the other brought expertise in estate planning.

Comment: This case clearly demonstrates two positive organizational consequences of turnover. First, attrition among habitual poor performers can be desirable. Second, and very importantly, this turnover can create the opportunity for infusing new knowledge and technology into the organization via the replacements.

H. Memorial Hospital has just received notification that it may lose its accreditation because of an insufficient number of registered nurses. Turnover among nurses continues to be high at the hospital; the problem is compounded by the departure of many area nurses from the profession and an insufficient flow of new nursing graduates into the region.

Comment: This example demonstrates the individual, organizational, and societal implications of turnover. Individuals are choosing to leave the hospital, and in some cases the profession. The effectiveness of the organization is suffering; consequently, the community is in danger of losing a needed health-care facility.

I. A U.S. Department of Defense executive ponders the testimony he is about to deliver to a congressional Armed Services Committee. Declining numbers of 18 to 25 year-olds in the United States during the 1980s and 1990s, combined with attrition rates of 30 to 40 percent during the first-term enlistment, could spell a threat to military staffing requirements and readiness.

> *Comment:* Turnover is not limited to the private sector. The attrition of military personnel, combined with the age demographics for the 1980s, poses important individual, organizational, and societal concerns.

J. The Executive Yuan of the Republic of China is asked to establish a study commission on employee turnover in Taiwan. With unemployment less than 2 percent and plans for continued rapid industrialization, an annual employee turnover rate of nearly 100 percent in many firms could have a disruptive impact on productivity growth and planned development.

> *Comment:* Employee turnover is not limited to the United States, as this case illustrates. With the continued multinationalization of business, understanding the cultural parameters of turnover is increasingly important.

K. Energy International's Board of Directors has just completed a review of the corporation's long-range strategic plan. Technological and capital constraints and acceptable contingency plans have been identified. The most significant constraint they found, however, concerned human resources. A continued high turnover in high-technology jobs, combined with a projected shortage of technical graduates in the next decade, resulted in a "red flag" on several potentially profitable new ventures. A task force of key executives was assigned to further evaluate the supply and turnover constraints and to report back with an options analysis within six months.

> *Comment:* Turnover analysis, together with labor-supply forecasts, is crucial in corporate planning. In this case, the combination of rapid turnover and insufficient supply of

high-technology graduates threatens otherwise lucrative business opportunities. A number of organizations have yet to effectively integrate corporate planning with detailed human resource analysis and planning.

L. The Corporate Vice-President of Human Resources for Fast Foods, Inc. just completed making his annual report to the Executive Committee. The fact that the annual turnover rate among food-processing employees continued to be 56 percent did not stimulate comment from the board. Of more interest were the facts that total labor costs had remained within budget and that applicant flow for vacant positions had remained strong. A nucleus of stable employees remained, and an adequate internal supply of assistant store managers could be identified.

Comment: In this particular organization, satisfactory applicants are readily available, training time is minimal, and control of labor costs is crucial. Given the current and forecasted environment of this organization, the relatively high level of food-processor turnover is not of strategic concern. The significance of turnover, from an organizational perspective, must be evaluated in the context of its environment and strategic plan.

Although many other examples could be given (and will be in subsequent chapters) these twelve cases serve to illustrate a number of fundamental points about employee turnover. These points include:

1. Turnover can have positive and negative implications for individuals, their careers, and their self-concept. It affects the "stayers" as well as the "leavers."

2. Turnover is potentially costly, and organizations need to document these costs carefully.

3. Turnover can have positive organization implications. It can, for example, create opportunities for promotion, infusing new ideas and technology, and displace poor performers.

4. Lack of turnover can create its own set of problems, such as blocking career-development paths, entrenching dated methods, and accumulating poor performers.

5. Turnover can have societal implications in such areas as health-care delivery, military readiness, and productivity and industrial development.

6. Turnover extends to countries other than the United States.

7. Turnover is important in strategic corporate planning.

These and other issues will be further developed in subsequent chapters.

THE SCOPE OF THE PHENOMENON

The preceding examples are illustrative. However, they do not sufficiently document the scope of the turnover issue. In this section data are presented suggesting that employee turnover is a pervasive phenomenon that cuts across type and size of organization, location, and time.

The Bureau of National Affairs (BNA) publishes a quarterly report on employee turnover. Table 1.1 summarizes the average monthly total separation rates for 1978–1980 by size and type of organization, and by region (BNA, March, 1979, 1980, 1981). The average monthly separation rate for all organizations was 1.9 percent for both 1978 and 1979, and 1.4 percent for 1980. Further, note the differences in separation rates by size, industry, and region in each of these three years. The lowest separation rates were in industries classified as manufacturing, in companies employing more than 2500 people, and in the Northeast. The highest separation rates were in smaller organizations, finance organizations, and the West.* We will explore these differences in later chapters.

The U.S. Department of Labor's Bureau of Labor Statistics (BLS) also publishes monthly turnover statistics by industry and

---

*The BNA quarterly turnover report is based on a national sample usually exceeding 500 organizations belonging to the BNA Personnel Policies Forum and/or the American Society Personnel Administration. Turnover rates are based on the number of total permanent separations (excluding temporary or involuntary layoff) during the month, divided by average number of employees on the payroll during the month, times 100. See BNA, March, 1980 for detailed sample description.

TABLE 1.1

Average monthly turnover rates as a percentage of average work-force: 1978—1980

	1978	1979	1980
By Number of Employees			
Up to 250	2.3	2.2	1.5
250—499	2.2	2.2	1.7
500—999	2.0	1.9	1.5
1000—2499	1.8	1.7	1.3
2500 and more	1.4	1.3	0.9
By Industry			
Manufacturing	1.8	1.6	1.3
Nonmanufacturing	2.0	2.0	1.6
Finance	2.4	2.5	2.0
Nonbusiness	2.1	2.1	1.7
Health care	2.3	2.2	2.0
By Region			
Northeast	1.7	1.6	1.3
South	2.0	1.8	1.5
North Central	1.9	1.8	1.8
West	2.4	2.4	2.2
All Companies	1.9	1.9	1.4

SOURCE: BNA's Quarterly Report on Job Absences and Turnover, 4th Quarter, 1978, 1979, 1980. Reprinted by special permission from *Bulletin to Management,* March 1979, 1980, 1981, by the Bureau of National Affairs, Inc., Washington, D.C.

region as a part of its regular Employment and Earnings series. The BLS report identifies "quits," "layoffs," and "total separations" (quits, layoffs, and all other separations) per 100 employees. The average monthly manufacturing quit rate has fluctuated over the past ten years — from an average monthly high of 2.8 percent in 1973 to a low of 1.4 percent in 1975 (BLS, 1980). As we will discuss in the next chapter, there is a clear relationship between level of unemployment and quit rate (Hulin, 1979, reports a .84 correlation over 31 years). For our purposes here, it is interesting to note that even in 1975 (with unemployment at 8.5 percent, the highest of the past decade) the average monthly quit rate was 1.4 percent — an annualized rate of approximately 16.8 percent. Looking at the problem from the management perspective, we must ask, who were the quitters, why did they quit, and what were the consequences.

Turnover is not limited to the private sector of the economy. As noted in case I in the preceding section, attrition is an important issue in the military. The attrition rates among first-term enlisted personnel in the four branches of the U.S. military have exceeded 30 percent per year for entering cohorts each year since 1973 (U.S. Department of Defense, 1978).* Over all branches, 35 percent of the 1977 enlistees did not complete their enlistment. It is interesting to note that the U.S. Air Force exhibited the lowest first-term enlistee attrition rates over the last decade. Are the differential attrition rates attributable to the "quality" of the entering recruits and/or to the nature of the work and organizational environment? This is the type of issue managers must address.

Case J above suggests that turnover is not limited to the United States. In a study of turnover among the Taiwan subsidiaries of thirty-nine large multinational organizations, the 1978 total separation rate was 99.5 percent among production workers and 20 percent among salaried and professional employees.† For discussions of turnover in other countries see, for example, Marsh and Mannari (1977), Japan; Van der Merwe and Miller (1973), South Africa; Moffatt and Hill (1970), Australia; and Chaplin (1968), Peru.

---

*The enlisted personnel attrition rates reported by the Department of Defense are based on cohorts. The attrition rates represent the percentage of accessions who failed to complete the first three years of their initial enlistment.

†Personal communication from Mr. E.H. Teng, Dupont Far East, Inc., Taiwan, 1979.

Turnover among shorter-tenure employees deserves special attention. Reviews of the turnover literature by Mobley, Griffeth, Hand, and Meglino (1979), Muchinsky and Tuttle (1979), Price (1977), and Porter and Steers (1973), indicate a consistent negative relationship between tenure and turnover. Endicott (1978) reports that 51.7 percent of the 1975 master's degree graduates left their employer within the first three years. As examples of specific occupations, Sorenson, Rhode, and Lawler (1973) document high early turnover among accountants in CPA firms, while the Conference Board (1972) discusses early turnover among salespeople. Wanous (1980) provides an important work directed toward understanding early adjustment by new employees. The fact that turnover is especially acute among shorter-tenure employees receives particular attention in subsequent chapters.

Other data documenting the pervasiveness of turnover are presented in later discussions. For the purposes of this introductory chapter, the data presented above serve to illustrate that turnover cuts across regions, organizations, nations, and time. The determinants and consequences of turnover and observed differences in turnover are a primary focus of the remainder of this book. Before proceeding, however, a general definition of employee turnover is presented and the perspective of the book is clarified.

DEFINING EMPLOYEE TURNOVER

The general definition of employee turnover used here is: *the cessation of membership in an organization by an individual who received monetary compensation from the organization.*

Several aspects of this general definition require comment. First, the focus is on *cessation* or separation from an organization and *not* on the related but distinct issues of accession, transfer, or other internal movement within an organization. (Note that accession and internal mobility will be discussed later as they relate to turnover.) Second, the focus is on *employees,* those who receive *monetary compensation* from the organization as a condition of membership. This book is not concerned with nonemployee relationships between individuals and organizations, e.g., students, volunteers, and union or fraternal membership. While turnover is an interesting and important issue in situations other than the employee-organization context, such turnover is beyond the scope of this book. Finally, this general definition of turnover is applicable to any type of organization — manufacturing, service, government, etc. — and is applicable to any type of employee-organization relationship arrangement, including part-time or full-time and hourly or salary arrangements. The controlling part of this definition is that the individuals receive monetary compensation for their membership in the organization. (For a useful discussion of alternative definitions of turnover and related concepts see Price, 1977.)

Given this general definition of employee turnover, it is possible to distinguish among various *types* of cessations. A frequently used distinction is between *voluntary* separations (employee-initiated) and *involuntary* separations (organization-initiated, plus death and mandatory retirement). The U.S. Bureau of Labor Statistics (1980) classifies separations in three ways: "quit," "layoff," and "other." These distinctions are deceptively simple. More definitive categories are needed. As will be discussed in detail in Chapter 3, the understanding and effective management of employee turnover requires definitive and reliable schema for measuring and classifying types of turnover.

A MANAGERIAL PERSPECTIVE

The preceding sections illustrate several basic implications of employee turnover and present data relevant to the scope of the phenomenon. Hopefully this introductory material will convince the manager or prospective manager (if such convincing is necessary) that employee turnover is a pervasive and important issue — one worthy of careful management attention.

A great deal has been written about turnover from a variety of perspectives including economic, psychological, sociological, management, accounting, personnel, and industrial relations. One need only browse through the bibliography of this book to appreciate the richness, in volume and perspective, of the turnover literature. Although a variety of sources and perspectives are utilized, the primary perspective of this book is managerial. The emphasis is on integrating the turnover literature and organizing the discussion in such a way as to be of direct benefit to the current or prospective manager.

What does this managerial perspective imply? The manager must be able to: *diagnose* the nature and probable determinants of turnover in his/her organization(s); *assess* the probable individual and organizational consequences of the various types of turnover; *design* and *implement* policies, practices, and programs for effectively dealing with turnover; *evaluate* the effectiveness of changes; and *anticipate* further changes required to effectively manage turnover in a dynamic world. Figure 1.1 summarizes this perspective.

The remaining chapters are directed toward developing this managerial perspective. Chapter 2 focuses on the positive and

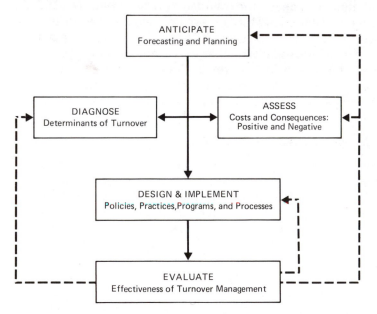

Fig. 1.1. *A management perspective of the turnover process.*

negative consequences of turnover, from both the organizational and individual perspectives. Chapter 3 deals with analyzing turnover within the organization, and Chapter 4 discusses a variety of approaches to controlling and effectively managing turnover. Note again that controlling and effectively managing do *not* imply elimination of turnover. Chapter 5 reviews the causes and correlates of turnover reflected in the current literature. Chapter 6 summarizes several models and presents an integrative model of the antecedents of turnover. Finally, Chapter 7 discusses gaps in our understanding, takes a look at the future, and emphasizes the pro-active, anticipatory management role.

A final note is warranted. Although the emphasis is on the managerial perspective, we hope that the individual reader will find the material useful in thinking about his or her own career planning and development.

Consequences of Turnover

2

INTRODUCTION

The bulk of the research on turnover has focused on causes and correlates. Relatively less attention has been devoted to the consequences of turnover (Dalton and Todor, 1978; Dalton et al., 1982; Mobley, 1980, 1982; Staw and Oldham, 1978; Staw, 1980; Steers and Mowday, 1981). Although many turnover researchers and writers acknowledge that "turnover is not all bad," most do not systematically deal with the individual or organizational consequences of turnover. Of the limited research that deals with turnover consequences, most has been directed toward estimating the costs to the organization.

In this chapter, we will explore a variety of individual and organizational consequences of turnover. As will become evident, the relative lack of research on turnover consequences permits few strong generalizations. However, a number of positive and negative consequences can be identified. If turnover is to be effectively managed, a fuller understanding of consequences is imperative. Further, measurement technology for assessing the net utility — that is, the overall consequences of turnover — is needed.

POTENTIAL NEGATIVE ORGANIZATIONAL CONSEQUENCES

Costs

The most frequently studied organizational consequence of turnover is monetary cost. Although the importance of measuring turnover costs has been emphasized for many years (see, for example, Gaudet, 1960) surprisingly few organizations make a systematic effort to evaluate the direct or indirect costs of turnover. Gustafson (see Appendix) observes that only rarely does a manager have more than the vaguest idea of how much it costs to replace an employee.

It serves little purpose to catalogue the turnover cost estimates from various studies since common estimation procedures are not used and most studies are unique to the organization, positions, and time-period studies. This does *not* minimize the importance of such studies or their potential value in management decision making. Rather, it simply means that until a common turnover cost system is broadly adopted, comparisons of cost estimates across studies or organizations are not particularly useful. Further, there is a dearth of research that captures the *quality* of the leaver or the replacement in the turnover cost estimation. Although replacement costs may be similar whether the leaver is a good or a poor performer, the true cost and consequences to the organization certainly differ as a function of the quality of the leaver and the replacement.

What is clear from studies of the cost of turnover is that turnover is expensive. A few examples will suffice. Gustafson (see Appendix) estimates that the Bell System replaces in excess of 100,000 employees yearly and that the outlay for personnel replacements is "unquestionably greater than $1,000 per occurrence" (p. 4). Mobley and Hall (1973) found that the turnover cost per 100 trainees during the first eight weeks of employment among operators in a fiber manufacturing operation was $98,500 (lost training investment plus replacement cost). Huck and Midlam (1977) estimate that the cost to the U.S. Navy to produce one high school graduate reenlistment approaches $100,000. This cost reflects expected attrition and reenlistment rates. Mirvis and Lawler (1977) estimate the turnover cost for bank tellers is in excess of $2,500 per quit.

Knowing that turnover is expensive is inadequate for effectively managing turnover. Gustafson (Appendix) suggests that high cost does not automatically mean that replacement of personnel is bad economics. Given the capital to make such action feasible, no rational businessperson would hesitate to make such an investment if it would increase productivity sufficiently to return a good profit on the investment. Dalton and Todor (1979) argue that to look at costs without considering benefits may lead to a distorted view of the utility of turnover. We will discuss potentially positive consequences later.

It is clear that a valid assessment of turnover costs must incorporate some concept of investment and unrealized return on that investment for leavers, investments, and expected return for replacements. Although the technology associated with such measurement is still being developed, the area of human resources accounting is helpful (Bassett, 1972; Brummet, Pyle and Flamholtz, 1969; Huck and Midlam, 1977; Flamholtz, 1974; Mirvis and Macy, 1976; Pyle, 1969) and provides a starting point.

Flamholtz (1973, 1974) presents models for measurement of original and replacement human resources costs. Figure 2.1 summarizes the "original costs," that is, the "sacrifice" incurred to acquire and develop human resources, divisible into direct and indirect acquisition and learning costs. "Replacement costs," Fig. 2.2, represent the sacrifice that would have to be incurred today to replace human resources presently employed and include costs attributable to the turnover of a present employee and the costs of acquiring and developing a replacement (see Flamholtz, 1974, p. 36).

Recruitment costs include advertising, travel, agency fees, campus recruiting, and administrative costs. Selection costs include interviewing, reference checks, testing, assessment centers, and related administrative costs. Hiring and placement costs include physicals, moving and travel, and related administrative costs. Learning costs include orientation, formal and on-the-job training, trainer's time, and lost productivity among other people during the training of a newcomer. Separation costs include the

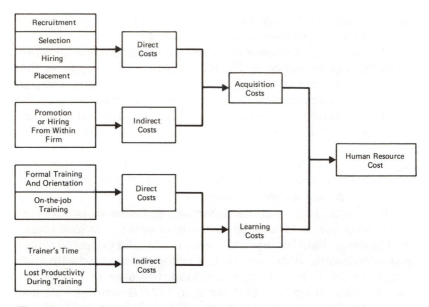

Fig. 2.1. *Model for measurement of original human resource costs*

Source: Flamholtz, E.G. *Human Resources Accounting* (Encino, Calif: Dickenson, 1974). Reprinted by permission of Dr. Eric G. Flamholtz.

costs of out-processing, separation pay if applicable, and the costs associated with a vacant position and any decrement in performance prior to separation. See Flamholtz (1974) for a number of examples utilizing these human resource costs.

Identification of original investment and replacement costs is important in estimating the cost of turnover. However, these figures are inadequate by themselves. For example, does the original investment appreciate (due, for example, to tenure-related benefit costs to the organization) or depreciate (due, for example, to obsolescence)? What is the expected service life of the individual? What is the expected return on the human-resource investment? Answers to these sorts of questions require consideration of factors beyond original investment and replacement costs, including other consequences of turnover

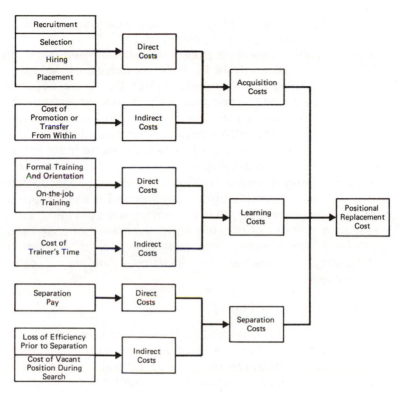

Fig. 2.2. *Model for measurement of human resource replacement costs*

Source: Flamholtz, E.G. *Human Resource Accounting* (Encino, Calif: Dickenson, 1974). Reprinted by permission of Dr. Eric G. Flamholtz.

and individual performance and potential. We will discuss such factors in later sections.

Flamholtz (1974) indicates that a few organizations have developed accounting systems for their *investments* in human resources while others have begun to account for the *replacement cost* of their human resources. It would seem imperative that organizations begin more systematic development of accounting systems relevant to human resource management. Developing valid estimates of the cost and consequences of turnover is one important use of such a system.

The Appendix presents a previously unpublished paper on work-force-loss cost analysis by H.W. Gustafson of American Telephone and Telegraph Company (AT&T). Gustafson cogently discusses both conceptual and pragmatic issues associated with developing a valid basis for assessing turnover costs. Gustafson's work, Flamholtz's (1974) book, and the developing literature on human resource accounting provide useful input for organizations that wish to develop valid turnover cost information.

An accounting approach to turnover costs is one important step toward more effective understanding and management of turnover. However, inspection of the components of Figs. 2.1 and 2.2 reveals a number of missing consequences that may influence the assessment of the organizational *utility* of turnover. In the following sections, we will discuss a variety of other consequences.

Disruption of Performance

As noted in Fig. 2.2, Flamholtz (1974) identifies two indirect performance costs associated with separation costs: loss of efficiency on the part of the leaver prior to separation, and cost of having a position vacant during the search for a replacement. However, other performance costs may be involved. To the extent that the leaver had unique skills and/or occupied a pivotal position, the loss may have a ripple effect on performance far beyond the vacant position, and this effect may continue until the replacement(s) become fully functional. To the extent that others must pick up the slack, their own performance may suffer. Further, depending on the quality of the replacements relative to the leavers, loss of high performers and/or high-potential individuals can have a lingering effect on the organization.

Disruption of Social and Communication Patterns

Formal and informal social and communication patterns are characteristic of any organization. If leavers are valued coworkers, if they are central in communication networks, and/or if the work group is cohesive, turnover can have negative effects on those remaining that go beyond additional work load and possible performance declines. Price (1977) suggests that turnover can have a negative effect on group integration and cohesion and that it can hinder the development of cohesion in groups experiencing high turnover.

Decline in Morale

Partly related to disruptions of performance and social and communication patterns, turnover may negatively affect the attitudes of those who remain. Turnover may by itself stimulate additional turnover by causing a decline in attitudes and by highlighting the fact that alternative jobs may be available (Staw, 1980). Thus employees who previously were not seeking alternative jobs may begin to search for them (Mobley, 1977). As will be noted in the section on individual consequences, the effects of turnover on the attitudes and behavior of those remaining are in part a function of the perceived reasons for others leaving (Steers and Mowday, 1981) and the relevance of others leaving for the remainers' performance, social support, and internal mobility (Mobley, 1982).

Undifferentiated Control Strategies

Another possible negative organizational consequence is that "undifferentiated" turnover control strategies and policies will be implemented. Since turnover is a visible behavior and since sufficient information on causes and consequences is frequently unavailable, management may respond with inappropriate, ineffective, and/or counter-productive responses. Across-the-board pay increases, "crash" human relations training for supervisors, organization-wide turnover goals of X percent, etc., are the types of undifferentiated strategies which may be inappropriate. An alternative is to take the managerial diagnostic and evaluative approach suggested earlier in Fig. 1.2. We will discuss the need for differentiated, data-based responses to turnover in greater detail in Chapters 3 and 4.

Strategic Opportunity Costs

Turnover can have a serious negative organizational effect by causing organizations to postpone or cancel potentially profitable ventures. For example, the author is working with a large energy resource company where the management committee is evaluating the need to cancel several new ventures, as a direct consequence of projected human resource constraints caused by turnover of key technical and managerial personnel. A hospital with which the author is working is having to delay opening a new wing because it cannot attract and retain nurses.

Given the tight labor market projected for many occupations over the remainder of the twentieth century, we can expect turnover to be a significant variable in strategic long-range planning. While estimation of opportunity costs is difficult, such costs are real.

POTENTIAL POSITIVE ORGANIZATIONAL CONSEQUENCES

Turnover is most frequently thought of in terms of negative organizational consequences. However, a number of authors have begun conceptual exploration of possible positive organizational consequences (Dalton and Todor, 1979; Mobley, 1980, 1982; Staw, 1980). The relative neglect of possible positive organizational consequences may be due to the fact that they may be less obvious and quantifiable and take longer to become evident than negative costs (Staw, 1980). In this section, we will explore possible positive organizational consequences. Again, strong generalizations are not possible given the dearth of empirical research.

Displacement of Poor Performers

Perhaps the most obvious positive organizational consequence is replacement with better performers. Performance of leavers is generally ignored in the turnover literature (Martin, 1981; Mobley, 1982), and practitioners too frequently fail to incorporate the performance of the leavers and stayers in their turnover analyses. In preparing this book, the internal-turnover analysis and reporting practices of a number of large U.S. companies were reviewed. Surprisingly few companies systematically assess the performance of leavers. This oversight needs attention. Given the increasing use of human resource information systems (see Chapter 5) the performance-turnover analysis is feasible. Further development of human resources accounting should lead to cost-benefit analyses regarding the expected utility of investing in attempting to develop and motivate poor performers versus encouraging turnover and investing in replacements.

In an interesting analysis of performance and tenure, Staw (1980) identifies three hypothetical functional relationships, shown in Fig. 2.3. He suggests that the "traditional" perspective assumes that performance of a new employee will initially be

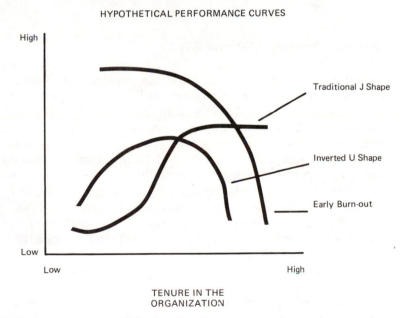

HYPOTHETICAL PERFORMANCE CURVES

Fig. 2.3. *Hypothetical performance curves*

Source: Staw, B.M. (1980). The consequences of turnover. *Journal of Occupational Behavior* **1**:253–73. Reprinted with permission of John Wiley & Sons, Inc.

low, will accelerate, and eventually reach a plateau — that is, a J-shape function. However, for stressful, physically demanding, or rapidly changing technology and knowledge jobs, an inverted-U performance curve may be more descriptive. Some jobs, especially service-oriented ones, may be characterized by high early performance and subsequent "burn-out." Staw argues that most jobs are characterized by the inverted-U performance curve and that greater attention should be devoted to studying the tenure and performance relationship so that the *appropriate* rate of turnover can be identified. This is a cogent argument. However, with increasing government regulation of age and broadly defined "handicapped" protected classes, the business necessity of any personnel decisions based on tenure-performance analyses should be rigorously evaluated and documented.

Innovation, Flexibility, Adaptability

Turnover creates opportunities for replacements, and such replacements may bring with them new knowledge, ideas, approaches, technology, and styles. Dalton and Todor (1979) and Staw (1980) discuss a number of ways in which turnover can contribute to organizational effectives via infusion of new technology, reorganization, variety, and disruption of entrenched bureaucratization. These potential benefits are a function of: the nature of the business; its technology; the quality of the replacements relative to the leavers; the position levels involved; opportunities for innovation and organizational change; and amount of turnover. Although Price (1977) does not find strong support for the proposition relating turnover and innovation, the indirect evidence is sufficient to warrant more systematic attempts to evaluate this relationship.

Turnover may present opportunities for cost reduction by eliminating or merging vacant positions, redefining jobs, and/or introducing new automation. Further, one strategy for overcoming resistance to organizational change — e.g., new technology, job enrichment, etc. — is to assure no elimination of positions except those that become vacant via turnover.

The issue of increased internal mobility is potentially a positive consequence of turnover on the individual level. From the organization's perspective, increased internal mobility creates flexibility in terms of career development and cross-training and may serve to increase morale among remainers.

Because it is visible and thought of as costly, turnover can in itself be a catalyst for positive organizational change, separate from the change that may be stimulated by replacements. In evaluating the causes and consequences of turnover, an organization may well evaluate and implement policies, practices, and processes that result in better turnover management and overall organizational effectiveness. For example, the organization that moves toward making salary increases contingent on results (see, e.g., Lawler, 1973; Mobley, 1974) may not only reduce turnover among better performers but also may enhance overall performance. Another example comes from a large energy company that has initiated several major "organizational development" efforts stimulated by concern with turnover. These "OD" efforts are having a positive influence on turnover as well as other areas of organizational functioning.

Decrease in Other Withdrawal Behaviors

It has been suggested that when individuals would like to quit their jobs, but are unable to do so (because of lack of alternatives, family constraints, etc.), they may engage in other forms of withdrawal such as absenteeism, apathy, sabotage, and poor quality work (Porter and Steers, 1973; Staw and Oldham, 1978; Steers and Mowday, 1981). To the extent that this is the case, it may be beneficial to the organization for such individuals to leave rather than incur the costs of such alternative forms of withdrawal. Again, cost-benefit analyses relating alternative forms of withdrawal, and strategies likely to be effective in countering such withdrawal, would be appropriate.

Reduction of Conflict

Staw (1980) identifies a potentially important consequence of turnover in his discussion of conflict resolution. He notes that much of the literature on conflict assumes that conflict can and should be arbitrated, resolved, or worked through in order for the organization to function effectively. Staw argues, however, that many personal or task conflicts are not easily resolved, especially if they stem from differences in fundamental values or beliefs; thus turnover may be the ultimate solution to the conflict. This author has seen this type of resolution recently following the merger of two organizations with very different managerial philosophies and styles. Not until turnover occurred among several key executives did effective functioning develop. To the extent that deeply ingrained conflict impairs organizational functioning, turnover as a last-resort means of conflict resolution may well be positive from both organizational and individual perspectives.

POTENTIAL POSITIVE INDIVIDUAL CONSEQUENCES

The individual who quits a job may be motivated by expectations of greater net positive consequences in a new job. This may be in the form of expected higher earnings, job challenge, career development, more supportive organizational climate, or a variety of other outcomes the individual may value. Alternatively, the individual may quit as an escape from a stressful work situation and/or a work situation that is not a rewarding person-organization fit. Such escape may well be a psychologically healthy step for the individual.

The individual who initiates a search for an alternative job and successfully locates one, or the person who is recruited by another organization, may experience greater self-confidence and efficacy. Successfully testing oneself in the job market can be reinforcing. Further, the challenge, variety, and stimulation associated with assuming a new job may be a personal catalyst for individuals who find these things lacking in their present job.

Schein (1978) argues that the career-development process has three interrelated components — self, job, and family. From the perspective of turnover, the individual may be motivated to quit for personal reasons, e.g., a desire to pursue nonwork values, to accommodate a spouse's career, or to move to a location where the children can get better public education. In agreement with Schein's thesis that we must consider the "whole person," it is clear that attempts to map the individual consequences of turnover must assess the self and family dimensions as well as the job dimensions. Such nonjob consequences may well be crucial to the expected positive consequences for the individual.

It is important to note that *expected consequences* are most relevant in the individual turnover decision process. Whether the actual consequences turn out to be what was expected is another matter which we will discuss in the next section.

While the considerations discussed above deal with positive consequences for the individual leaver, turnover also may have positive consequences for individuals who remain. As noted in the discussion of organizational consequences, turnover can create internal mobility opportunities. To the extent that the individual stayers are good performers with potential, their upward mobility may be enhanced. To the extent that individuals who left were not valued or were disruptive, satisfaction and cohesion among the individuals who remain may be enhanced. Further, the induction of high-quality replacements may serve to stimulate, cross-fertilize, and/or revitalize those who remain.

Steers and Mowday (1981) and Mowday (1981) were among the first to begin a systematic conceptual and empirical exploration of the psychological processes associated with how individuals remaining with the organization perceive, evaluate, and respond to others leaving the organization. How do they reconcile their remaining with the fact that valued others leave? How does the supervisor respond to the loss of valued employees? Answers to these important questions are worthy of increased attention.

POTENTIAL NEGATIVE INDIVIDUAL CONSEQUENCES

In the previous section we suggested that individuals who leave probably expect a net positive consequence. However, individuals frequently have inaccurate and/or incomplete information about the organizations they are about to join (Wanous, 1980). Further, individuals may mentally justify or rationalize the decision to leave the former employer, for example, by establishing excessively high expectations about the chosen alternative (Steers and Mowday, 1981). Schneider's (1976) reference to "the grass is greener phenomenon" is a descriptive label. To the extent that the leaver has unrealistic expectations, the encounter with the reality of the new organization may lead to disillusionment and negative attitudes. Thus the expected net positive consequence of moving could in reality end as a net negative consequence; that is, the grass is not greener after all.

The same phenomenon could describe job mobility that is primarily motivated by concerns not related to work — for example, a desire to move to a new region or to adopt a new life style. Moving to the sunbelt, or taking a job in a small town for family reasons, involves many personal uncertainties. The subsequent encounter with reality may or may not satisfy expectations. The attitudinal and behavioral consequences of unfulfilled expectations, related to the job itself or not, would be a function of the extent to which important values were involved (Porter and Steers, 1973; Locke, 1976).

Other possible negative consequences exist for the individual. Quitting may involve loss of nonvested benefits, seniority, and associated perquisites. Recently there have been inflation-related costs of geographic mobility. A prime example is replacing a relatively low-interest mortgage with one bearing double-digit interest.

Moving and changing jobs can be stressful. To the extent that one misjudges this stress and/or is not equipped to cope with it, the net consequence may be negative. Relatedly, the disruption of social relationships for both the individual and family can have negative consequences.

Another factor is the increased numbers of dual-career families. Movement by one spouse may have a disruptive effect on the other spouse's career development (Schein, 1978). If the job change was motivated by escape from a bad job situation, the alternative may or may not be consonant with an individual's career aspirations.

It could be argued that the individual evaluates potential negative consequences relative to expected positive consequences before quitting. However, given the uncertainty associated with an individual accurately anticipating the positive and negative consequences of changing jobs, there would seem to be little question that the net consequence will be negative for some individuals. As Hall (1976), Schein (1978), and Wanous (1980) suggest, organizations can do a great deal to help current and prospective employees make better career choices, at a minimum by making available more detailed and accurate information. We will develop this issue further in Chapter 4.

Turnover can have negative as well as positive consequences for the individual stayers (Steers and Mowday, 1981). Some of these negative consequences include loss of coworkers who were valued either for instrumental job-related and/or social-interpersonal reasons; increased personal workload; having to learn to deal with the replacement; and loss of a boss on whose "coattails" one was riding. Again, research is just beginning to deal systematically with postturnover individual consequences and processes (Steers and Mowday, 1981; Mowday, 1981).

SOCIETAL CONSEQUENCES

Although a detailed discussion of societal consequences of turnover is beyond the scope of this book, such consequences require some comment. As with individual and organizational perspectives, societal consequences can be positive or negative. From a positive perspective, labor migration to newer or expanding industries is necessary for continued economic development; migration to higher paying industries can increase per-capita income; workers leaving jobs they find stressful may reduce the societal costs associated with psychological and physical manifestations of stress; the lack of mobility, especially in declining labor markets, may increase societal costs for unemployment and welfare (Dalton and Todor, 1979).

Examples of possible negative societal consequences are also evident. The economic impact on a community associated with plant closings or inability to attract new industry is well recognized. What is not frequently discussed is that the inability to attract and retain a competent work force is one reason for this loss of industry or inability to attract new industry. For example, in the late 1960s the Delmarva peninsula on the East Coast was experiencing such high levels of employee turnover and migration of the younger portion of the work force that productivity and growth in the region were impaired.

Excessively high levels of turnover can increase the cost of production and can even result in idle productive capacity due to lack of trained operators, as was the case in the textile industry in the early 1970s.

Whether one classifies these sorts of consequences as positive or negative depends on one's frame of reference, time perspective, and socio-economic perspective. Just as management can no longer ignore the societal impact of the organization on the physical environment, they cannot ignore the impact of the organization on the societal human resource environment. To do so is to invite even more government intervention.

Turnover Utility Analysis

The preceding chapter documents a variety of causes and correlates of turnover. This chapter has discussed a variety of cost and other possible negative, as well as positive, consequences of turnover. From a management perspective, what is needed is a mechanism for evaluating the *net utility* to the organization of turnover — that is, a means of integrating the positive and negative costs and consequences of turnover for individuals at differing levels of position, performance, and potential (Mobley, 1982).

This is crucial for collecting valid management information on turnover costs and consequences. Further, there is a management need to relate the effect of changes in causes of turnover — such as behavioral intentions, job satisfaction, organizational commitment, etc. — to this net utility index.

The human resource accounting literature discussed earlier has made progress toward measuring original investment and replacement costs. However, indexing the variety of other potential positive and negative turnover consequences and an adequate incorporation of individual performance and potential are still needed.

Relating turnover costs and consequences to causal variables is in an early state of development. Likert (1973) and Mirvis and Lawler (1977) present a methodology for relating attitudinal and cost data. Their method involves using the correlation between attitudes and cost data to predict the effect of attitude changes in cost terms. Mirvis and Lawler (1977), for example, estimate that an increase in job involvement from a −.5 standard deviation to a +.5 standard deviation from the mean among tellers in a midwestern bank would reduce turnover costs from $27 to $7 per teller per month. While the methodology used in this study does not disclose the multiple causes and correlates of turnover, it does represent a good start toward developing means of relating causes and consequences of turnover.

Further development of the measurement technology associated with estimating the utility of turnover, and relating utility to changes in causal variables, should be one of the priority goals of turnover researchers and human resource practitioners.

SUMMARY

Relative to causes of turnover, consequences have been underemphasized. Recently a number of authors have begun to address more systematically the conceptual and empirical issues associated with turnover consequences (e.g., Dalton and Todor, 1979; Mobley, 1982; Price, 1977; Staw, 1980; Steers and Mowday, 1981; Mowday, 1981). Table 2.1 summarizes some of the possible

TABLE 2.1
Examples of possible positive and negative consequences of employee turnover

ORGANIZATION	INDIVIDUAL (LEAVERS)	INDIVIDUAL (STAYERS)	SOCIETY
Possible Negative Consequences			
—Costs (recruiting, hiring, assimilation, training)	—Loss of seniority and related perquisites	—Disruption of social and communication patterns	—Increased costs of production
—Replacement costs	—Loss of nonvested benefits	—Loss of functionally valued coworkers	—Regional inability to keep or attract industry
—Out-processing costs	—Disruption of family and social support systems	—Decreased satisfaction	
	—"Grass is greener" phenomenon and subsequent disillusionment		
—Disruption of social and communication structures		—Increased workload during and immediately after search for replacement	
—Productivity loss (during replacement search and retraining)	—Inflation-related costs (e.g., mortgage cost)	—Decreased cohesion.	
—Loss of high performers	—Transition-related stress		
—Decreased satisfaction among stayers	—Disruption of spouse's career path	—Decreased commitment	

−Stimulate "undifferentiated turnover control strategies

−Career-path regression

Possible Positive Consequences

+Displacement of poor performers

+Infusion of new knowledge/technology via replacements

+Stimulate changes in policy and practice

+Increased internal mobility opportunities

+Increased structural flexibility

+Decrease in other "withdrawal" behaviors

+Opportunities for cost reduction, consolidation

+Reduction of entrenched conflict

+Increased earnings

+Career advancement

+Better "person-organization fit," thus less stress, better use of skills, interests

+Renewed stimulation in new environment

+Attainment of non-work values

+Enhanced self-efficacy perceptions

+Increased internal mobility opportunity

+Stimulation, cross-fertilization from new coworkers

+Increased satisfaction

+Increased cohesion

+Increased commitment

+Mobility to new industry

+Reduced income inequities

+Reduced unemployment and welfare costs in a declining labor market

+Decreased job stress-related costs

positive and negative consequences of turnover. This table is not exhaustive, the cells are not mutually exclusive, and a given consequence is contingent on a number of other variables. However, this table and the preceding discussion serve to illustrate that it is simplistic to think of turnover in terms of any single consequence.

Progress toward understanding turnover consequences and integrating such understanding into more effective turnover management requires further development in at least two areas. First, additional conceptual and empirical research on specifying organizational, individual, and societal consequences and processes such as that initiated by Staw (1980), Steers and Mowday (1981), and Dalton and Todor (1979), respectively, is needed. Second, further development of human resource accounting and human resource measurement technology is required so that the various positive and negative consequences can be integrated into some form of net utility index. Flamholtz (1974), Mirvis and Lawler (1977), and Gustafson (Appendix) are laying groundwork. However, more attention to measurement and integration of costs and consequences, and to relating such utility estimates to predictors of turnover, are required for effective management of turnover.

(We encourage the reader to read the Appendix, *Force-Loss Cost Analysis,* by H.W. Gustafson, at this point.)

Analyzing Turnover

3

INTRODUCTION

In this chapter we discuss a variety of turnover-analysis measures, tools, and techniques. Given the relative lack of strong generalizations of turnover causes and consequences, organizations must conduct regular, systematic internal analyses. The chapter starts with a discussion of overall measures of turnover rates and the need for multiple measures and multi-level categorizations. Analyzing the relationships between turnover, performance, and potential is emphasized as well as the need to analyze turnover by Equal Employment Opportunity (EEO) category. This is followed by a discussion of: measuring employee perceptions, attitudes, and expectations; exit interviews; relating attitudes to turnover costs; and analyzing turnover consequences.

MEASURING TURNOVER RATES

Turnover rates are generally expressed as a percentage for a specified period of time. Like any other percentage, turnover rates are a function of what goes into the numerator and denominator. A variety of rates are reported, many not directly comparable and each tapping a different aspect of turnover. Tracking and comparing appropriately constituted turnover rates can be useful for management. However, care in constructing and comparing such rates is crucial if valid inferences are to be drawn. Several different rate measures will be required. In this section, we will examine several of the most useful turnover indices from a management perspective. For treatment of a wider range of indices, see Byrt (1957), Gaudet (1960), Price (1977), and Van der Merwe and Miller (1971).

Separation Rates

Perhaps the most frequently used turnover (separation) index is:

$$TTR = \frac{S}{N} \times 100 \tag{1}$$

where:

TTR = Total turnover rate

S = Number of total separations in the time interval, e.g., month or year

N = The average number of employees on the payroll of the unit being studied. This can be an average of the daily or weekly number on the payroll or simply the number on the payroll at the beginning of the period plus the number at the end of the period, divided by two.

A major problem with this formula is that it does not specify the reasons for separation.

A more useful approach is to divide separations into categories such as voluntary quits, discharge for cause, layoffs, deaths, retirement, and other. While the denominator would remain the same for whatever time period studied, the numerator would differ.

$$QR = \frac{Q}{N} \times 100 \tag{2}$$

where:

QR = Voluntary quit rate

Q = Number of quits

N = Average number on payroll during the period being studied

$$DR = \frac{D}{N} \times 100 \tag{3}$$

where:

DR = Discharge for cause rate

D = Number of discharges

N = Average number on payroll during the period being studied

$$LR = \frac{L}{N} \times 100 \tag{4}$$

where:

LR = Layoff rate

L = Number of permanent layoffs

N = Average number on payroll during the period being studied

The Department of Labor's Bureau of Labor Statistics, in its *Employment and Earnings Series,* breaks out rates by quits, layoffs, and other.

An even more useful managerial approach is to further divide reasons for separation into specific categories. Table 3.1 gives one set of categories adapted from a major aerospace company. Note that turnover rates attributable to each category can be calculated and that categories can be combined to form summary quit rates, discharge rates, etc. The key to this level of specificity is getting valid reasons for individual turnover. We will discuss this issue later in this chapter.

Survival and Wastage Rates

The various separation rates discussed above, while useful, suffer from several sources of ambiguity. As Van der Merwe and Miller (1971) suggest, a 100 percent annual separation rate could indicate that: the entire work force has turned over; half the work force turned over twice; a quarter of the work force turned over four times, etc. Further, as Price (1977) suggests, the various separation rates do not control length of service — one of the more consistent negative correlates of turnover.

To deal with these shortcomings, an organization should supplement the tracking of various separation rates with survival

TABLE 3.1
A major organization's reason for turnover categories

DISSATISFACTION:
Wages—amount
Wages—equity
Benefits
Hours or shift
Working conditions
Supervision—technical
Supervision—personal
Coworkers
Job security
Job meaningfulness
Use of skills and abilities
Career opportunities
Policies and rules
Other: _____

ALTERNATIVES:
Returning to school
Military service
Government service
Starting own business
Similar job: same industry
Similar job: other industry
Different job: other industry
Voluntary early retirement
Voluntary transfer to subsidiary
(loss of seniority)
New position:
  Organization
  Position
  Location
  Earnings

LIVING CONDITIONS:
Housing
Transportation
Child care
Health care facilities
Leisure activities
Physical environment
Social environment
Education opportunities
Other: _____

ORGANIZATION INITIATED:
Resignation in lieu of dismissal
Violation of rules, policy
Unsatisfactory probation period
Attendance
Performance
Layoff
Layoff: downgrade refused
Layoff: transfer refused
End of temporary employment

PERSONAL:
Spouse transferred
To be married
Illness or death in family
Personal illness
Personal injury
Pregnancy

OTHER:
Transfer to: _____
Leave of absence from: _____
On loan to: _____
Retirement
Death

and wastage rates. These rates focus on cohorts (groups of employees) that enter the organization in a given time period, and track their turnover.

$$WR = \frac{Li}{N} \times 100 \tag{5}$$

where:

WR = Cohort wastage rate

Li = Number of leavers in the cohort with specific length of service i

N = Number in the original cohort, e.g. all 1980 hires

$$SR = \frac{Si}{N} \times 100 \tag{6}$$

where:

SR = Survival rate

Si = Number of stayers in the cohort with specified length at service i

N = Number in the original cohort

Survival rate is the complement of cumulative wastage rate.

Table 3.2 is an example of wastage and survival rate calculations. Assume International Electronics hired 500 new engineers in 1978. If a hundred left during the first six months, the wastage rate would be 20 percent (100 ÷ 500). If seventy more left during months 7 to 12, the wastage rate for this interval would be 14 percent (70 ÷ 500). The survival rate at the end of the first year would be 66 percent (330 ÷ 500). In our example, the wastage rate by 1981 among the 1978 cohort of new engineers is 53 percent. Endicott (1978) reports that the three-year wastage rate for the 1975 cohort of MBA graduates was 51.7 percent.

The U.S. Civil Service Commission (1977) found that in any given cohort of hires, from two-thirds to three-fourths of all the quits will occur by the end of the first three years; of these, more than half will occur by the end of the first year alone. The U.S. Civil Service Commission (1977) has developed a computer program, available from the U.S. Government Printing Office (see bibliography), for analyzing the tenure-turnover relationship. This program is useful for many organizations.

TABLE 3.2

An example of wastage and survival rate calculations

Length Of Service (Months)	(N=500 New Hires In 1978 Cohort)			
	Number Of Leavers With Specified Length Of Service	Number Of Stayers With Specified Length Of Service	Internal Wastage Rate	Cumulative Survival Rate
6 months or less	100	400	20.0	80.0
7 to 12	70	330	14.0	66.0
13 to 18	40	290	8.0	58.0
19 to 24	30	260	6.0	52.0
25 to 30	15	245	3.0	49.0
31 to 36	10	235	2.0	47.0

External Comparisons Using Turnover Rates

In making comparisons between an organization's turnover rates and various externally reported rates, it is important that the same type of rates, e.g. quit rate, layoff rate, etc., are being compared. It is equally important to make comparisons as specific as possible with respect to industry, occupation, region, and time. Unfortunately, comparative data, cross-tabulated with this level of specificity, are difficult to obtain, although the U.S. Department of Labor's Bureau of Labor Statistics reports industry breakdowns by SIC codes and by quit, layoff, and total separation rates in its *Employment and Earnings* series. While the Bureau of National Affairs (BNA) reports total separation rates by general type of industry, size, and region, it does not report quit rates or cross-tabulations.

INTERNAL ANALYSIS OF TURNOVER RATES

From a managerial perspective, analyses and external comparisons of an organization's overall quit and turnover rates are only a starting point. Breaking down turnover rates by a variety of individual and organizational variables is necessary for turnover diagnosis.

Table 3.3 suggests a number of variables which may be useful in the internal analysis of turnover. Depending on the objective of the analysis, subdividing turnover by any one of these variables could be useful. However, turnover is too frequently analyzed in terms of only one variable at a time. Analyses that involve combinations of variables potentially related to turnover will have much greater diagnostic value.

The increasing use of computer-based human resource information systems makes regular analysis and reporting of turnover, cross-tabulated by multiple variables, feasible. Regular turnover management reports, as well as special turnover research analysis, are important uses of such information systems. This author advocates such systems, given the increased government reporting requirements, the need for more effective human resource planning, and the need for prompt and reliable human resource information retrieval. For the employer without such a system, manual cross-tabulation of turnover rates by selected multiple variables is still feasible.

The list of variables in Table 3.3 is not exhaustive and the particular set of variables analyzed would depend on the management need and/or the personnel research question at hand.

TABLE 3.3
Useful variables in internal analysis of turnover rates

Position	Tenure	Performance
Department	EEO-1 category (race-ethnic-sex)	Potential
Supervisor	Biographical data	Values and expectations
Shift	Education—level	Attitudes
Location	Education—type	Career expectations
Unit	Earnings	Behavioral intentions
Division	Earnings history	Reason for separation
Function	Absenteeism	Follow-up perceptions
Source	Job history	

However, several variables are given particular attention in subsequent sections, including performance, EEO categories, and employee perceptions, attitudes, expectations and intentions.

TURNOVER BY PERFORMANCE AND POTENTIAL

Throughout this book, we emphasize the importance of relating turnover to performance and potential. In Chapters 5 and 6 we suggest that the turnover research literature has inadequately addressed this relationship and that many organizations fail to analyze it. Yet the organizational consequences of turnover are dependent on *who* leaves and *who* stays (see Chapter 2; Gaudet, 1960; Gellerman, 1974; Staw, 1980). The departure of poor performers with low potential may be an opportunity for replacements with higher performance and potential. On the other hand, the loss of high performers with potential, where equivalent replacement is less likely, may have significant negative consequences for the organization.

Figure 3.1 shows one of a series of performance and turnover analyses — this one between divisional quit rate and performance — conducted by a large multidivisional organization. In this case, the quit rate (overall and in two of three divisions), was greater among high-performing professional employees than among lower performers. This situation clearly requires additional diagnosis. Cross-tabulating by tenure, position, location, reason for quitting, and other relevant variables would facilitate the diagnosis. In addition, it is important to identify why turnover is lower among high performers in Division C. Much can be learned about the individual and organizational causes and correlates of turnover by detailed analysis of such differences. Finally, analysis of overall turnover rates, ignoring performance of leavers, could potentially be misleading.

Reliable and valid measurement of performance and potential continue to require research and management attention (Landy and Farr, 1980; DeCotiis and Petit, 1978; Borman, 1978). However, analyses of turnover in terms of broad categories of performance and potential are feasible and essential if turnover is to be understood and effectively managed.

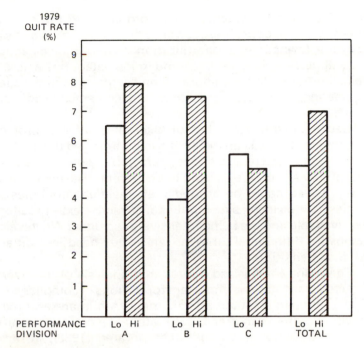

Fig. 3.1. *Professional employees quit rate by performance and division.*

TURNOVER AND EEO

Employers are under continuing pressure to increase their use of protected-class individuals (Holmes, 1980). The Federal Executive Agency *Uniform Guidelines on Employee Selection* (Equal Employment Opportunity Commission *et al.,* 1978, 1979, 1980) and the Office of Federal Contract Compliance's *Federal Contract Compliance Manual* (U.S. Department of Labor, 1979) emphasize statistical representation of minorities and females. Although the various government guidelines and statistical indexes may be criticized (see for example, Abram, 1979; Mobley, 1974, 1980; Morris, 1978; Sharf, 1979), they clearly must be addressed.

Turnover is related to EEOC-OFCCP concerns in at least two ways. To the extent that females and minorities are quitting (or otherwise being separated from) the organization, turnover may adversely influence progress toward affirmative action goals and contribute to apparent underutilization in various job categories. This will be especially troublesome in job categories where the availability of qualified minorities and females is limited (e.g., engineering, crafts, etc.), and where replacements are difficult to attract.

Second, to the extent that turnover rates differ for protected classes versus caucasian males, it could be argued that practices in the organization (e.g., pay treatment, job assignment, supervisory attitudes, etc.), are causing this differential turnover rate. Of course it also could be argued that qualified minorities and females have an increasing number of attractive external alternatives available and are being intensively recruited. Whatever the reasons for differential turnover rates, they need investigation and documentation.

The point emphasized here is that analysis of turnover by protected-class status is important for reasons of compliance and effective human-resource management. A human-resource information system can greatly facilitate this type of analysis. For example, Information Science Incorporated (1980), in its *Expanded EEO Compliance System,* includes analysis and reports of separations for various combinations of race, sex, age, job, grade, occupational category, EEO category, organizational unit, and reason for separation. Whether or not the organization has a computerized information system, such analyses are important management tools.

Where differential or excessive turnover rates exist, further diagnosis and documentation of the causes and steps to deal with the causes, should be implemented.

ASSESSMENT OF EMPLOYEE PERCEPTIONS, ATTITUDES, AND EXPECTATIONS

The literature on turnover discussed in Chapter 5 and the conceptual models presented in Chapter 6 document the relevance of a variety of employee perceptions, values, attitudes, and expectations to the turnover process. The organization's analysis of turnover should include a diagnosis of these variables. The Mobley *et al.,* (1979) model of the turnover process presented in Chapter 6 suggests that the following five general categories of variables need to be measured from the employee's perspective:

1. Job satisfaction;

2. Expectations and evaluation of alternative jobs outside the organization;

3. Expectations and evaluation of alternative jobs inside the organization;

4. Nonwork values and roles and their relation to job behavior;

5. Turnover behavioral intentions.

We will discuss the diagnostic use and measures of each of these general categories.

Job Satisfaction

The relationship between job satisfaction and turnover, although not particularly strong, is consistent. Dissatisfied employees are more likely to leave than satisfied ones. The fact that the relationship is not stronger does not suggest that satisfaction should not be measured. It does suggest that measures of satisfaction must be combined with other measures to effectively predict and understand turnover.

A number of standardized measures of job satisfaction are available — The Job Descriptive Index, JDI (Smith, Kendall, and Hulin, 1969); The Minnesota Satisfaction Questionnaire (Weiss, *et al.,* 1967); The Job Satisfaction Index (Brayfield and Rothe, 1951). In addition, a number of research and consulting firms market standardized and/or semi-standardized employee attitude surveys (for example, Opinion Research Corporation and Science Research Associates). Finally, organization-specific survey measures can be designed internally and/or with the assistance of consultants or university personnel.

The employee attitude and satisfaction survey can be a useful diagnostic tool *if* it is well designed and validated; it is administered under conditions where employees feel safe in giving candid responses; and if employees are given feedback and can see positive results from participating in the survey. (See Dunham and Smith, 1979, for a detailed discussion of organizational surveys.)

Job content is one dimension that previous research has shown to be a significant contributor to both satisfaction and turnover for many individuals. A useful measure of how employees perceive and evaluate the content of their jobs is the Job Diagnostic Survey, JDS (Hackman and Oldham, 1975). This standardized measure assesses task variety, task significance, task identity, autonomy, and feedback, as well as several individual difference and satisfaction variables.

Particularly useful are employee surveys that measure the various dimensions of satisfaction, such as pay, job content, supervision, coworkers, and working conditions. Further, periodic readministering surveys permit analysis of changes and trends. Greater use of longitudinal rather than "snapshot" analyses is an ongoing need in turnover research.

Expectations and Evaluations of Future Internal Roles

Job satisfaction is present- and past-oriented. Analyses of the causes of turnover must also include assessment of employee expectations and evaluations of their future within the organization. Do employees expect their jobs to improve or deteriorate? Do their jobs contribute to their career aspirations? What are employees' expectations regarding promotion and transfer opportunities? Detailed assessment of such future-oriented employee expectations and evaluations are infrequently included in turnover studies. Conceptually, a strong case can be made for giving more attention to this category of variables. We will discuss this further in the next chapter section on career planning and management.

Alternatives Outside the Organization

The model of employee turnover presented in Chapter 6 emphasizes the role of the individual's perception and evaluation of alternative jobs outside the organization. In a free and competitive labor market, employees will periodically assess alternatives through highly visible advertising, movement of acquaintances, and/or informal communications. Although a dissatisfied employee, or one with "fast-track" career aspirations, may be more likely to search for and evaluate alternatives, the satisfied employee and the employee expecting rewarding internal career mobility will periodically be attracted by alternatives. Thus it is important that an organization periodically assess how it is evaluated relative to other employers in the labor market. This can be accomplished both through interviews and surveys of employees, and through direct assessment of labor market competition.

Many organizations do a regular and systematic analysis of their wage and salary structures relative to their industry and labor market(s). As noted later, this is an important activity. Managers need valid salary survey data on both the industry and the relevant labor markets in order to effectively price their own salary structure. The same logic applies to other factors related to the organization's ability to attract and retain competent employees.

Variables other than wages and salaries have been related to turnover. Although an organization's wages may be competitive, it may lose competent employees because they perceive other employees as having more meaningful job content, more promotion opportunities, more flexible hours, more supportive supervision, and better working conditions. Just as an organization should assess competitive salary survey data, it should also evaluate the competitiveness of nonwage factors associated with attracting and retaining competent employees.

Exit and follow-up interviews and surveys among leavers; employee surveys; surveys of representative individuals in the relevant labor market; and periodic evaluation of competitors' human resource policies and practices are potentially important sources of analytic data in turnover diagnosis and action planning.

Nonwork Factors

Nonwork values, such as leisure or location preferences, can contribute to turnover and/or interact with job-related variables in influencing turnover. In addition, family responsibilities, dual-career families, and conflict between work and nonwork roles, can have an impact. Analysis of the causes of turnover must extend beyond job-related factors.

Nonwork factors can be assessed via: employee interview and survey procedures, exit interview and follow-up data, evaluation of the relevant labor market or potential additions to the labor force, and the scheduling, transfer, and other policies of other employers. We will discuss diagnostic questions and turnover management implications related to nonwork factors in the next chapter.

Behavioral Intentions

One of the best individual predictors of turnover is the employee's stated intention to stay or leave. Questions regarding employees' intentions to remain for the next six or twelve months, can be imbedded in other employee attitude and satisfaction measures. Such behavioral intention statements are helpful diagnostics and can be used in human resource planning and forecasting models (see Kraut, 1975; Mobley, 1977; Mobley *et al.,* 1978).

EXIT INTERVIEWS AND FOLLOW-UP ON LEAVERS

The exit interview has been used for a long time as one source of information on the reasons for turnover. While we recommend its use, we must recognize that the exit interview in itself is an inadequate source of data for turnover analysis. Employees who are about to leave the organization: may be reluctant to be candid, not wanting to "burn their bridges" behind them; may give only socially acceptable responses; and/or may have developed rationales to justify their leaving which do not reflect their original or most salient reasons for leaving.

To be effective, the exit interview, like other forms of interviewing, should be structured and conducted by trained interviewers in an atmosphere that encourages the candor of the departing individual.

For additional input, organizations should consider using follow-up surveys among former employees. Through the follow-up survey one can assess the reliability of exit interview data. Further, it gives one the opportunity to assess whether or not the former employee's expectations and evaluations of the new role, relative to the previous job, are being realized. Schneider (1976) notes the "grass looks greener" phenomenon may be a part of the turnover decision process.

In the case of both the exit interview and the follow-up survey, the organization may wish to consider using an outside resource, such as a consultant or university personnel. Such outside individuals can guarantee anonymity to respondents and may prove a more neutral recipient of critical information. Follow-up surveys can also be done by internal personnel. A major oil company gets a 60 percent return rate on its follow-up surveys.

Cohort Analysis

A particularly useful analysis technique is to track cohorts of employees and periodically compare leavers and stayers within various groups. Examples of cohorts might be engineers hired in a given year, female managers, management trainees, etc. By administering periodic surveys and/or interviews, and subsequently comparing stayers and leavers, the organization can identify the variables (such as perceptions of pay, job content, career expectations, etc.), and changes in variables associated with turnover. Cohort analysis provides a "moving picture" of employee perception, attitudes, and expectations rather than a "snapshot" of a cross-section of employees at a given point in time.

RELATING ATTITUDES AND COSTS

In Chapter 5 we document the relationship between turnover and certain employee perceptions, attitudes, and intentions. In Chapter 2 we discussed the costs and consequences, both positive and negative, associated with turnover. A recurring issue in human resource management is how to express employee attitudes and behavior in monetary terms. As noted in Chapter 2 and Appendix A, some progress has been made in estimating the investment costs associated with employee acquisition and replacement (Flamholtz, 1974; Gustafson, Appendix A). However, relating such turnover costs to attitudes and behavior, and changes therein, are important additional concerns.

From a managerial perspective, relating changes in employee attitudes, perceptions and intentions to the monetary consequence of turnover would be highly useful for cost-benefit analyses of policies, practices and programs designed to change perceptions, attitudes, and behavioral intentions. A number of researchers (Likert, 1973; Likert and Bowers, 1973; Myers and Flowers, 1974; and Mirvis and Lawler, 1977), have developed approaches which are partially responsive to this issue.

Drawing on the literature at the time, Mirvis and Lawler (1977) reasoned that job satisfaction and involvement should be among the best attitudinal predictors of voluntary turnover. Turnover costs were estimated using acquisition, replacement, and overhead costs (Macy and Mirvis, 1976). By establishing the statistical relationship between employee attitudes and the probability of turnover, it is possible to crudely estimate the turnover cost savings associated with a given change in attitudes (see Mirvis and Lawler, 1977, for details on the methodology).

While this approach is an important beginning in the attempt to link changes in attitudes to turnover costs, a number of conceptual and measurement problems remain unsolved. The Mir-vis and Lawler approach does not cover the performance of leavers or possible positive consequences of turnover. For example, Dalton (1980) suggests some conditions under which turnover has positive cost savings implications. Further, the statistical equations used to relate attitudes and probability of turnover do not capture the multiple attitudes and expectations needed to predict turnover. Additional work is clearly needed to develop methodologies for linking attitudes and job behavior to turnover and its costs. However, progress in this area will significantly improve managerial decision-making and evaluation.

ANALYZING CONSEQUENCES

In Chapter 2 we discussed a variety of positive and negative consequences of turnover. An internal organizational analysis of turnover must go beyond an evaluation of causes of turnover to include an analysis of its consequences. In Chapter 2, Appendix A, and the preceding section we discuss several approaches to developing cost estimates. However, existing cost models are insufficiently sensitive to the variety of possible turnover consequences, both positive and negative. The lack of a common metric for indexing the utility of turnover is a continuing problem.

At this time, it is not possible to present a measurement system for aggregating the variety of turnover consequences. However, recognizing the variety of consequences, such as those suggested in Table 2.1, and developing procedures for estimating the separate, if not aggregate costs of various positive and negative consequences, are necessary and feasible.

The author has worked with a manufacturing organization that established a multi-division task force to develop cost-estimation procedures for turnover consequences. Representatives from manufacturing, accounting, industrial engineering, information systems, and personnel, with their unique perspectives, can make significant progress in developing estimation methodology that will be useful in managerial decision-making.

In addition, the task force served a useful organizational development function in bringing together multiple components of the organization to work on a problem of common concern.

SUMMARY

In this chapter we presented a number of general approaches to the analysis of turnover rates, causes and consequences within the organization. It should be evident that meaningful analysis requires more than computation of aggregate turnover rates and exit interviewing — perhaps the primary analytic approaches in many organizations.

The approach suggested here calls for detailed analysis of turnover by position, performance, EEO category, tenure, location, supervisor, reason, and other classification categories listed in Tables 3.1 and 3.3. Analysis should include both separation and wastage rates. Sources of data on causes include: personnel records, regular employee surveys, exit interviews, follow-up surveys of employees who leave, and competitive analyses to include factors in addition to monetary compensation. Tracking cohorts that enter the organization at the same time through periodic surveys or interviews and comparing stayers and leavers can be particularly useful diagnostic techniques. Surveys and interviews should assess not only present job perceptions and attitudes, but also expectations regarding the individual's career, perceptions of alternative jobs, nonwork values, and intentions to stay.

Only after valid diagnostic information on the causes, correlates, and consequences of turnover has been gathered, can effective turnover management and control strategies be designed. Possible control strategies are the subject of the next chapter.

Controlling Employee Turnover

4

INTRODUCTION

In this chapter we focus on some of the ways management can effectively control turnover. Once again we emphasize that the term "control" does not mean undifferentiated attempts to minimize turnover. In Chapters 2 and 3 we discussed a variety of instances where turnover can have positive organizational and individual consequences. Used here, control means: effectively managing turnover; encouraging turnover where it will have net positive consequences; and seeking to minimize turnover where it will have net negative consequences.

This chapter could easily be a multiple-volume encyclopedia on effective human resource management. Given the complex, multi-faceted nature of turnover, there are obviously no panaceas or pat prescriptions for managing turnover. Space does not permit a detailed treatment of all the possible approaches to effective turnover management. A fundamental point, made several times already, is that management responses to turnover must be based on diagnosis and evaluation of the causes and consequences of turnover in the context of the organization. Our objective here is to focus on some of the areas that may need more effective turnover management. For each area, we suggest several diagnostic questions. Data for answering these diagnostic questions come from the analytic tools and sources discussed in Chapter 3. The areas selected for emphasis in this chapter are: recruitment, selection, and early socialization; job content; pay practices; supervision; career management; alternative work schedules; and other opportunities for effectively managing turnover.

RECRUITMENT, SELECTION, AND EARLY SOCIALIZATION

The processes by which individuals choose and are chosen for jobs offer a number of important opportunities for more effective turnover management. Wanous (1980) argues that the organizational entry process is one of *matching* the individual and organization (p. 10). This matching is based on: individual aptitudes and abilities relative to job requirements; and individual values, preferences, and expectations relative to organizational norms, policies, practices, rewards, and conditions. As noted below, this matching is an ongoing process since both individuals and organizations are constantly changing.

The traditional approach to the matching process is based on the organization's assessment of the individual relative to organizational and job requirements. Standardized tests, work samples, interviews, weighted application blanks, biographical inventories, are among the traditional employee selection techniques which, when validated, may be useful selection techniques (Arvey, 1979).

The literature reviewed in Chapter 5 suggests that these traditional employee selection techniques can predict turnover. Although the ability of individual tests to predict turnover is not particularly strong, when such predictors are used in combination they are important to turnover management.

Given the increasingly complex government guidelines on employee selection (see Arvey, 1979), many employers have abandoned systematic employee selection. However, in instances where recruitment, training, and replacement costs are high; and where the costs of selection errors are high (for example, in seniority-based job progression systems and potentially dangerous settings), the continued development of valid predictors of turnover is worthwhile. In such instances, the author continues to be a strong advocate of validating and implementing traditional selection techniques.

If this matching process is to be effective, both the individual and the organization must be actively involved (Wanous, 1980; Porter, Lawler, and Hackman, 1975). Too frequently prospective and new employees have inaccurate information and unrealistic expectations. Wanous (1980) summarizes conceptual and empirical evidence that *realistic* recruitment and selection can enhance the matching process, increase satisfaction, and reduce voluntary turnover.

The realistic job preview (RJP) is one way an organization can enhance realism. Not a single technique, the RJP is rather "a general philosophy or approach" (Wanous, 1980, p. 83). This philosophy or approach assumes that giving candidates and newcomers accurate and complete information will result in better matching, increased satisfaction and commitment, and lower turnover. The realistic information can be transmitted through booklets, films, video-tape, realistic work samples, interviewers, supervisors, other recent hires, and a combination of these approaches.

Figure 4.1 presents Wanous's (1978) model of how the realistic job preview influences turnover through: "vaccination" against negative aspects of the organization; increased self-selection; and enhanced commitment to the choice of the organization.

Horner (1979) found that the RJP, given *after* organizational entry, could be an effective mechanism for increasing role clarity and teaching coping skills, also components of the Wanous model. Both Horner (1979) and Wanous (1980) review the literature on RJPs and turnover and conclude that the RJP can help reduce employee turnover. While much remains to be learned about the psychological processes involved, the RJP is one approach worthy of management consideration in effective turnover management.

The time immediately after entering the organization is important in shaping employee attitudes and behavior. The new employee should be provided with: accurate expectations of

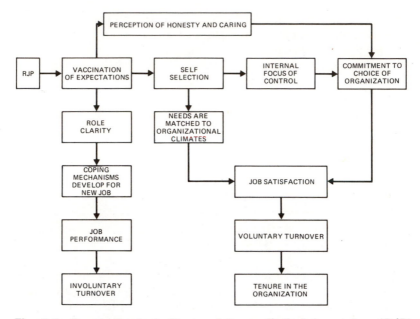

Fig. 4.1. *Psychological effects of the realistic job preview (RJP).*

Source: From J.P. Wanous (1978). Realistic job previews: Can a procedure to reduce turnover also influence the relationship between abilities and performance? *Personnel Psychology* **31**:251. Reprinted by permission of publisher and author.

what the job requires and the organization expects; a clear understanding of reward contingencies; and assistance in establishing a social support system among peers, the supervisor, and others. Such early socialization may take several months. This sort of systematic early socialization is substantially different from the traditional several-hour orientation program.

Many organizations have a probationary period as a matter of policy or contractual agreement. Yet the probationary period frequently is not effectively used. To be effective, the probationary period should provide systematic evaluation and feedback to the new employee, "mentoring," coaching and counseling, and joint employee-employer evaluation of the probable success of a continuing employment relationship. The probationary period can be considered an extended job trial. Where the organization and/or individual conclude there is a mismatch, individualized training and development, transfer, or termination may be appropriate. Given the fact that employee selection and early socialization procedures will not result in perfect matching, early transfer or termination of some individuals will be inevitable and desirable from both individual and organizational perspectives.

Turnover is higher among new employees. To the extent that recruiting, training, and replacement costs are high, this early turnover may represent *negative utility* for the organization. To the extent that the individual leaves the job with a sense of failure and/or a sense of time wasted or opportunities forgone, this early turnover may represent negative utility for the individual as well.

Conversely, early turnover can also represent *positive utility.* Turnover may be desirable among individuals who are unable to work effectively, to benefit from training and development opportunities, and/or to either adapt to or change the norms of the organization.

Given the fact that both individuals and organizations change; given the current state of our ability to measure and effectively match individuals and organizations; and given the fact that early turnover may be positive or negative, it would be naive to assume that the recruitment, selection, and early socialization processes are *the* answer to effective turnover management. However, there should be little argument that these processes are important for effective turnover management and are underdeveloped in many organizations.

Diagnostic questions relevant to recruitment and selection and early socialization include the following:

1. Is early turnover evident?

2. Can mismatches in aptitude and ability be identified?

3. Are new employees entering the organization with unrealistic expectations?

4. Does the recruiting and selection process include means for transmitting realistic job information?

5. Have selection techniques been validated with turnover criteria?

6. Has the utility of employee selection techniques been evaluated?

7. Does the organizational entry process include mechanisms for teaching coping skills, communicating role expectations and reward contingencies, and building social support systems?

8. Has an effective probationary period been developed that includes systematic evaluation, feedback, coaching and counseling?

JOB CONTENT

In our summary of the literature presented in Chapter 5 we suggest that employee perceptions and evaluations of job content are one of the more consistent correlates of turnover. In Chapter 3, we suggested the Job Diagnostic Survey, JDS, Hackman and Oldham (1975) as one useful analytic tool for assessing employee perceptions and evaluations of their job content. Figure 4.2 presents the Hackman and Oldham model. To the extent that employees value tasks with meaningfulness, identity, significance, feedback and variety, designing jobs with such qualities should enhance satisfaction with job content and decrease turnover.

Mobley (1976) uses an analogy between work and golf to illustrate several points about job design. To the extent that: goals are unclear; feedback is indirect or delayed; variety is diminished through high specialization and routinization; and accountability, discretion and self-control are minimized, games like golf, and many jobs, will become boring or frustrating to those individuals who seek task meaningfulness and identity.

Not all individuals value an "enriched" job and the redesign of all jobs is not feasible. Thus the issue is one of effectively matching individuals' abilities, interests, and values with task and organizational requirements. This may be accomplished in

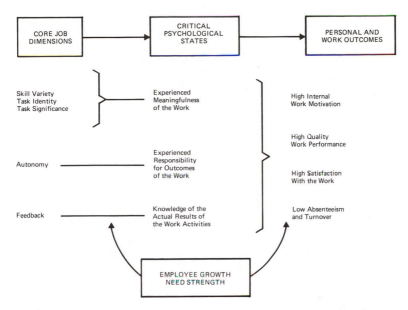

Fig. 4.2. *The job characteristics model of work motivation*

Source: From J.R. Hackman and G.R. Oldham (1975). Development of the Job Diagnostic Survey. *Journal of Applied Psychology,* **60**:159–170. Copyright (1975) by the American Psychological Association. Reprinted with permission of the publisher and author.

two nonmutually-exclusive ways: selection- and placement-based strategies (tests, interviews, realistic job previews, job trials); or job design strategies. As the average education and expectations of the work force increase; as work values move toward a stronger desire for meaningfulness; and as selection ratios become less favorable in the tighter labor markets projected for the remainder of the century, job design strategies may take on added significance.

The employer with employees or applicants who value task meaningfulness needs to address this issue or face recruiting and turnover problems in the form of alternatives available to employees. Industries whose profit margins do not permit wage competition in a given labor market may find that meaningful jobs will be an effective way of competing in the labor market. The author worked with a small midwestern metals fabricator who was able to compete in this manner in a labor market dominated in numbers and wages by the automotive industry.

Sample diagnostic questions in the area of job content include:

1. Do employees (and applicants) value task meaningfulness and identity?

2. Is dissatisfaction with job content related to turnover in this organization?

3. Is job redesign feasible?

4. Would job redesign make the organization more competitive in the local labor market?

5. Are the costs and consequences of turnover such that turnover is preferred to the costs/benefits of job redesign?

COMPENSATION PRACTICES

The research summarized in Chapter 5 indicates that organizational differences in pay rates are related to turnover rates. While this relationship is far from perfect and does not address the individual-level prediction of turnover, it is apparent that organizations must continue to assess the competitiveness of their wages and benefits in the relevant labor markets. Salary surveys are widely used for this purpose and need not be detailed here.

Several caveats are, however, noteworthy. In regions experiencing an in-migration of new industry, e.g., certain sunbelt states, an employer must *anticipate* the impact of the new industry on the local market. Advance management assessment of the impact of the wages and benefits of new industry permits timely evaluation of strategies to address the new competition. To wait until after the new industry arrives risks disruptive levels of employee migration. The author has seen a number of examples of this phenomenon, particularly in smaller sunbelt towns. In one case, it took a division of a large corporation twelve months to get approval to adjust its salary scale after a new employer moved into the local labor market. During this interval, some 40 percent of the work force migrated to the new industry.

A second caveat centers on the need to keep informed of wage competitiveness and supply and demand in particular occupational categories. In certain labor markets, an inadequate supply for occupations such as systems analyst, programmer, petroleum engineer, or skilled craftsperson, may exert occupation-specific wage pressure. In such cases, managers must assess the need to adjust wages for such occupations even if not warranted by the internal job evaluation. Accelerated salary-growth curves for scarce occupations may be warranted.

In highly competitive geographical or occupational labor markets, management must have the flexibility to move quickly with respect to salary competition. The author observes that some large corporations, with highly centralized and standardized compensation systems, can find themselves at a competitive disadvantage because of the lag-time in responding to changes in regional or occupational labor markets.

Where an employer is unable to be wage-competitive in the market, careful attention must be given to other factors, such as job content or supervision, which allow the employer to recruit and retain a competent work force.

Internal Equity Considerations

Modern compensation theory and practice is increasingly cognizant of the importance of not only competitiveness of compensation relative to the labor market but also employee perceptions of internal equity in compensation across jobs within the organization. A well-developed and well-understood job evaluation process is important for internal equity. Job evaluation procedures are well-documented in a number of sources and will not be discussed here.

Among the consequences of increases in the minimum wage, competition for new college graduates in disciplines like engineering and accounting, and a tight labor market in certain entry-level positions, is pay *compression* among new employees and employees who have been in the organization for several years. Continuing inflation and the decline in the availability of young people in the coming decade may exacerbate the compression problem. The perception of inequity among those experiencing this compression can contribute to turnover if alternatives are available. Attempts to minimize this compression, as well as other forms of perceived inequity, are difficult but important in controlling turnover.

Pay, Performance and Turnover

If pay is a reward valued for what it will buy and/or for what it signifies (for example, recognition, attainment, status, etc.), and if individual performance is measurable and employee-controllable, then making a strong link between pay increases and performance may be a useful motivational strategy (Lawler, 1973, 1981; Mobley, 1974). Given recent levels of inflation, many individuals will be dissatisfied with the *absolute* amount of their pay increases. However, pay can still have a positive influence if the *relative* amount of pay increase is related to performance.

A relevant managerial question concerns *who* is dissatisfied with their pay — the good or the poor performers? Many managers argue for across-the-board increases. The effect of this undifferentiated reward policy is to reward incompetence and penalize competence. The poor performer is signaled that performance is not relevant to pay. Although dissatisfied with the amount of the increase the poor performer is reassured that (s)he got the same as everyone else.

The good performer also is signaled that performance is not relevant to pay. Also dissatisfied with the amount of the increase the good performer may be further dissatisfied that his/her good performance was rewarded in the same way as the poor performer. The good performer's response may be to lower performance or, if alternative jobs are available, to quit. As noted previously, the consequences of turnover are significantly different for good or poor performers.

The argument is not that pay is the only important reward, but that pay is the most tangible organizationally-controlled reward and thus is a potent signal. Failure to give greater rewards to good rather than poor performers may contribute to turnover among those individuals an organization would least like to lose. This is not to minimize the problems with validly measuring performance (Borman, 1979; Landy and Farr, 1980). However, too frequently managers may avoid establishing the pay-performance contingency even when performance can be adequately categorized for differential reward.

Sample diagnostic questions in the area of compensation include the following:

1. Are systematic salary surveys conducted to assess competitiveness in relevant labor markets?

2. Are regular and systematic job evaluation programs being conducted?

3. Are timely salary adjustments made in response to particularly competitive occupations?

4. Is the impact of new industry in the area being anticipated?

5. Where wage competition is not feasible, are alternative competitive strategies developed?

6. Are wage-compression problems being addressed?

7. Are the performance and earnings of leavers versus stayers being analyzed?

8. Does a performance-contingent pay increase policy exist?

9. Do employees see the link between pay increases and performance?

10. Are high-performance leavers less satisfied with pay practices than stayers?

Supplementary Benefits

A competitive supplementary or fringe benefit package may contribute to attracting and retaining employees. The increasing percentage of total payroll costs devoted to such benefits dictates that they be well-managed. The competitiveness of an organization's benefits can be assessed via benefit surveys in a manner similar to salary surveys. However, it is important to recognize that it is the employee's *perception* of the competitiveness of the benefits that controls the influence on turnover. If benefits are competitive, the organization should communicate this fact.

The concept of "cafeteria" benefit plans under which employees are able to choose, within limits, how they wish to allocate their benefit dollars, is conceptually appealing. Such plans allow better matching of employee values and needs with benefit options. Although such plans have not been widely adopted, perhaps due to concern about possible administrative costs, they continue to be worthy of consideration.

Benefits with an extended vesting period are one way to discourage turnover. However, with increased government and competitive pressures to reduce vesting periods, this may be an increasingly ineffective strategy.

A fundamental problem with benefits, from a turnover perspective, is that generally they are not performance-based. Thus they are available to all employees or to the employees in various broad categories, such as exempt, non-exempt hourly, salary executive, etc. As such, a highly competitive benefit plan may serve to discourage turnover among habitual poor performers. To the extent that this is the case, the organization may find it useful to consider diverting a portion of the total benefit cost to benefits or rewards that are performance-contingent. The effect would be both to reward good performance and to discourage turnover among good performers.

Sample diagnostic questions in the area of turnover and benefits include:

1. Are benefit plans competitive?

2. Do employees perceive the competitiveness of the benefit plan?

3. Would "cafeteria" benefit plans increase the value of benefits to individuals and the organization?

4. Can a portion of the benefit-loading be diverted to performance-contingent rewards?

LEADERSHIP AND SUPERVISION

Employee value attainment and rewards, fundamental to employee attachments to the organization, can come from several sources. As previously discussed, job content is a primary source of intrinsic reward, that is, attainment of such values as task meaningfulness and identity, while compensation is the most tangible form of extrinsic reward. However, the immediate supervisor also can be an important source and facilitator of employee reward and value attainment and can play an important role in turnover management.

The supervisor controls a significant reward — *praise* (Latham and Wexley, 1980). Given the time-demands on many supervisors, inadequate attention is given to the basic, yet important, supervisory task of praising employee performance. When supervisor-employee interaction is analyzed, we frequently find that supervisors spend more time criticizing than praising employees and their performance. An established principle of reinforcement theory is that the source of reinforcement and the situation surrounding positive reinforcement — in this case, the supervisor giving praise — builds positive attachment to the source and situation. Training supervisors in the effective use of praise and positive reinforcement is worth exploring from both work-motivation and turnover perspectives.

To the extent that the supervisor establishes a positive personal relationship with employees; demonstrates consideration for the employee; and creates a supportive environment, the employee may become less likely to quit because of personal attachment to the supervisor. While personal relationships between supervisor and employee are desirable, there are at least two risks involved. If the employee's sole attachment to the organization is through the supervisor and the supervisor changes, the employee's attachment to the organization may diminish. Thus multiple attachments must be developed. In addition, development of strong personal employee-supervisor relationships should not interfere with the supervisor's responsibility for critically evaluating performance, differentially rewarding based on performance, and developing high performance expectations and goals. Both risks can be managed and do not offset the advantages of building positive supervisory attachments.

Another way in which the supervisor can contribute to effective turnover management is to be a facilitator of employee task attainment. By creating conditions where achievement is possible, by providing feedback and recognition, and by removing obstructions to performance, the supervisor contributes to both task accomplishment and reward. Third, the supervisor must establish contingencies for the rewards (s)he controls. The supervisor who fails to develop an environment where goal attainment is valued and rewarded may be contributing to turnover among the potentially better performers. Further, the failure of the supervisor to establish reward contingencies may be reinforcing poorer performers who should either be trying to improve their performance or seeking other internal or external roles.

The supervisor can also play an important role in the early socialization of new employees (Graen, 1976). The supervisor is a primary source of role information, role expectations, feedback, and social support for the new employee. Important supervisory activities with respect to new employees include aiding the new employee by: reducing the ambiguity of the new situation; teaching the formal and informal cues, norms, and communications networks; clarifying and negotiating goal and reward expectations; and shaping new employee behavior by reinforcing successively closer approximations to desired role behavior. Supervisory training and development activities devoted to effectively managing the role-learning and assimilation of new employees is worthy of exploration in many organizations.

The supervisor plays an important role in employee training and career development. Through open discussion with employees regarding their training needs and career aspirations, and working to create appropriate training and development opportunities, the supervisor can facilitate the internal development of employees and enhance their future-oriented attachment to the organization.

Supervisors occasionally play a far too passive role in employee training and development. Training may take employees away from the job and developmental activities may hasten employee transfer or promotion. From the supervisor's perspective, these outcomes may be considered undesirable. To counter this, organizations must establish clear goals and reward contingencies for the supervisor's role in training and development of subordinates. Further, the organization must provide support for supervisors with policies, practices, procedures, and training which permit attainment of the objectives discussed in the preceding paragraphs.

Among the diagnostic questions in the area of supervision are the following:

1. Are supervisors developing a supportive work environment?

2. Are supervisors facilitating employee task attainment?

3. Are supervisors establishing reward contingencies?

4. Are supervisors trained in effectively managing the role-learning and assimilation of new employees?

5. Are supervisors active participants in the training and development of subordinates?

6. Is the organization providing supervisors with procedures, training, and rewards for accomplishing the preceding objectives?

CAREER PLANNING AND DEVELOPMENT

The Mobley, *et al.* (1979) model of turnover argues that turnover is related to present satisfaction and to future expectations and evaluation of jobs and roles within and outside the organization. For employees who value learning and/or refining skills and ability, and who seek to improve their job performance, organizationally-supported training and development can contribute to job satisfaction. Further, some economists argue that organization-specific training can serve to decrease mobility by building organizational-specific, but externally nontransferable, knowledge and skills (Becker, 1964).

Although employees may be satisfied with their present job, they may leave because they do not anticipate satisfying future roles. In addition, valued employees may become more prone to quit as changes evolve in their career path, personal aspirations and values, and family life. We characterize the recruitment and selection process in an earlier section as a matching process. However, this matching process extends beyond initial selection and can be considered ongoing throughout an employee's career (Schein, 1978).

Schein (1978) argues that this matching process is not the sole prerogative of the organization, but of the individual as well. Further, Schein (1978) suggests that the career-planning and development process must recognize the following multiple dimensions:

1. The total and changing person must be considered, that is, self-development, career-development, and family-development, and their interaction over time (p. 6);

2. Career paths and sequences and their interaction within occupations and within the organization must be analyzed and understood (p. 7);

3. Organizational-development efforts must be combined with explicit career-development programs (p. 9);

4. The culture or climate of the organization must be analyzed and understood in relation to career success and development (pp. 10–11);

5. Societal changes must be understood and reflected in career-development processes (p. 12).

In more specific terms, the organization needs to provide individuals with: accurate information on possible career paths; accurate feedback on their assessed potential on various career paths; opportunities for valid self-assessment; rewards for self-development; and developmental opportunities and programming. Broad-based job-posting systems; career and personal counseling; assessment centers; regularly updated career interest; expectation and location preference modules in the human resource information systems; reward systems for subordinate development; integration of strategic planning, human resource planning, and career development processes; are among the important components of a viable career-planning and development process.

It is important to recognize that a viable career-planning and development process which includes continuing joint employee and organizational assessment of probabilities of success along various career paths, will in some instances stimulate turnover. To the extent that changing self, career, family, and/or organizational needs suggest a mismatch has or is developing, turnover can be the best outcome for the individual and the organization.

It is also important to recognize that a currently satisfactory match between individual and position need not be disrupted in the name of development or upward mobility. Some individuals may decide that further upward mobility is not desirable. To the extent that the individual is competent in the present role and that the career development of a significant number of other employees is not being blocked, this may be a perfectly acceptable organizational outcome. The point is that organizations operating under the "up or out" philosophy should reexamine the cost-benefit of this philosophy.

Related to the career-development process is the growing need for retraining associated with an organization's changing technology and/or business. As industries mature, diversify, and develop new ventures, the mix of human resource knowledge skills, and abilities can shift. The oil industry is a good example. As emphasis develops in synthetic fuels, new and diversification ventures, fewer people may be required in the traditional businesses, such as retail marketing and refining. While encouraging turnover is one response to these changes, retraining is another.

To the extent that the labor market is tight for individuals needed to staff the changing or new businesses, it may be cost-effective for the organization to retrain valued employees who would otherwise be displaced. For employees who have acquired a great deal of organizational knowledge and demonstrated competence, retraining in areas needing new people may be effective. For example, retraining refining engineers in exploration or synthetic fuels or retraining marketing personnel in accounting or computer systems may be cost-effective. A number of universities are equipped to assist in such retraining ventures.

Finally, we emphasize that it is the individual's values, expectations, and perceptions of internal development opportunities that guide their turnover decision. Although the organization may have a rational career-development path outlined for the individual, if the individual does not perceive and positively evaluate this path, turnover may be the outcome. Further, a positively-evaluated career path at one point may not be evaluated so later. There is no alternative to a continuing and two-way dialogue between individual and organization if the career-planning and development process is to be effective.

Space does not permit a detailed discussion of the human resource planning and career-development processes. We direct the reader to Walker (1980) and Schein (1978) for two recent and highly useful references.

Among the diagnostic questions in the area of career planning and development are the following:

1. Are employees actively involved in their own career planning?

2. Are opportunities for self-assessment, information on career possibilities, and rewards systems for self and subordinate development provided?

3. Are high performers or high potentials leaving for lack of career-development information or opportunities?

4. Is the career-development process based on a continuing, on-line system that reflects constant changes in individual and organizational needs?

5. Does development programming match development planning?

6. Is an undue emphasis on upward mobility or geographic developmental transfers causing unwanted turnover of competent but nonmobile individuals?

7. Is the cost-effectiveness of retraining being evaluated relative to turnover in light of the organization's changing technology or business?

ALTERNATIVE WORK SCHEDULES

Rotating shifts, fixed nonday shifts, and/or inability to work full time may cause some individuals to seek other jobs or to not apply. This fact, combined with anticipated decreases in the younger-age cohort of the population and labor force, (Drucker, 1980; Wachter, 1980) may dictate that more organizations consider alternative work schedules. Some parents might welcome working a partial shift while children are in school or a half-shift at night after the children are in bed; some students might prefer working partial shifts around their classes; some retirees might welcome partial work schedules; some individuals might find part-time moonlighting an attractive supplement to their income. Organizations unable to recruit sufficient numbers of off-shifts might consider using more partial-shift employees.

Flexible hours and alternatives to the eight-hour, five-day week, also may be valuable in recruitment and retention. Such flexibility is consistent with individual differences in values and with seeking feasible and effective ways of accommodating such individual differences. While such flexibility in hours and shifts is far from a national trend, the majority of organizations adopting such procedures express satisfaction (Nollen, 1980). These same organizations may find a competitive advantage in the labor market.

Whereas almost 60 percent of the families in this country have two or more wage earners, organizations will increasingly be confronted with the need to examine the impact on recruitment and retention not only of work schedules, but of benefits such as paternity leaves, day-care centers, and transfer policies. (See *U.S. News and World Report,* June 16, 1980, for examples of how various U.S. companies are addressing this need.)

Finally, organizations which use part-time employees must recognize that the determinants of turnover may differ from those for full-time employees (Peters, Jackofsky, and Salter, 1981). Different policies and practices may be necessary to recruit and retain competent part-time employees.

Some possible diagnostic questions with respect to alternative schedules include:

1. Are employees leaving because of shifts, hours, or schedules?

2. Are insufficient full-time replacements available in the relevant labor market?

3. Is there a pool of partial-schedule workers in, or potentially in, the labor market?

4. Would flexible hours and/or alternatives to eight-hour shifts be compatible with the organization's technology and be valued by employees?

5. Would such alternative work schedules give the organization a competitive advantage in the labor market?

6. If part-time employees are used, will differential policies and practices be necessary for recruitment and retention?

OTHER OPPORTUNITIES FOR EFFECTIVE MANAGEMENT OF TURNOVER

The topics selected for discussion in this chapter represent some of the primary opportunities for more effective turnover management. Diagnosis within the organization will indicate which areas are worthy of relative emphasis. The diagnosis may suggest opportunities for more effective management of turnover other than those discussed above. While space limitation precludes detailed discussion, several are worthy of comment.

Security

Organizations that are subject to fluctuation in employment levels may experience difficulty in retaining employees due to fear of layoff. Some unions have attempted to address this issue by negotiating supplemental unemployment benefits. The author is aware of several nonunionized firms that have created a "security fund" which is used to buffer economic layoffs by offering paid vacations to senior employees, thus keeping lower seniority employees on the payroll. Job sharing is an alternative; the reduced scheduled work hours are shared among employees, thus minimizing layoffs. Security funds or job sharing may serve to buffer some of the impact of economic downturns and thus may help reduce the turnover contribution of job security. Obviously, careful study of the economic implications of such strategies is required before implementing.

Working Conditions

The physical work environment cannot be overlooked. The increased regulation, publicity, and general awareness of safety and environmental conditions, together with the aging of this nation's physical plants, lead to the hypothesis that working conditions will be an increasingly important factor in the recruitment and retention of employees. Work environments which are physically and psychologically safe and desirable are a worthy goal from turnover as well as broader organizational and societal perspectives.

Team Building

Just as job content, the supervisor, organizational goals, etc., can be sources of attachment to the organization, so can be the immediate work group and the "extended" work group with whom the individual employee interacts. The literature on team building that has developed recently should be of interest to the organizations seeking more effective turnover management (see Woodman and Sherwood 1980).

Centralization

Price's (1977) review concludes that highly centralized organizations experience greater turnover. This relationship may be based on such factors as less autonomy, less involvement in decision-making, slower response time to unit and individual needs, and/or perceived lack of control.

The structure of an organization is based on many factors, including technology, size, and rapidity of change in relevant external environments. However, high turnover may be one sign that the centralized structure is having dysfunctional consequences. In assessing organizational structure, turnover should be considered.

Communications

More effective communication with employees is widely advocated but unevenly practiced. Price (1977) suggests that both formal-organizational communications and task-specific communications are determinants of turnover. Developing direct and frequent task-specific feedback and multiple, frequent, and credible channels of formal communication are worthy objectives. Management attempts to improve the flow of communication should have positive organizational consequences in the area of turnover.

Organizational Commitment

The individual's belief in and acceptance of the goals and values of the organization is a major part of organizational commitment (Mowday, *et al.,* 1979). Such goal and value identification serves as another focus of attachment to the organization. This identification can be enhanced by a clear specification of the rationale of organizational goals and values, sharing the rewards of organizational goal attainment, and involvement in goals processes.

Encouraging Turnover

In the preceding sections we have suggested a number of areas that, based on diagnosis, may be useful in reducing undesirable turnover. Implicit in this discussion is the desire to retain valued employees. However, in Chapters 2 and 3, we described a number of positive consequences of turnover. In cases where turnover

has a positive net utility, it should be encouraged or accommo-
dated. Effective out-placement services, career counseling,
cost-benefit analysis of turnover versus retraining or replacement, are important in the process of managing turnover. Fundamental to knowing the net utility of turnover is an assessment
of the performance, potential, and replacement labor market for
the employees in question. As already noted, performance, potential, and replacement costs are too infrequently incorporated
in turnover analysis.

SUMMARY

In this chapter we have briefly discussed a number of areas
where organizations may find opportunities for more effectively
managing turnover. Given the multiple causes and consequences of turnover, no single policy, practice, or procedure will
be sufficient. Effective management of turnover requires examination of the entire human resource management process, including recruitment, selection, early socialization, job design,
compensation, supervision, career planning, working conditions
and schedules.

What is required is: regular and systematic diagnosis of
turnover; specification, and implementation of multiple
strategies; and evaluation of the utility, the cost-benefits of turnover and turnover management strategies. The diagnostic questions presented in this chapter, combined with the analytic and
data-gathering tools discussed in the preceding chapter, should
provide a basis for systematic diagnosis.

Causes and Correlates of Turnover

5

INTRODUCTION

The primary objective of this chapter is to call to our attention the variables related to turnover as shown by previous research. This focus should assist the manager or personnel researcher in formulating *hypotheses* about the causes and correlates of turnover in the organization(s) to be studied.

Even with the extensive amount of previous turnover research, relatively few strong generalizations are possible. As we will discuss later in this chapter, our current inability to make stronger generalizations is related to: the paucity of research examining multiple possible causes and correlates of turnover in the same study; failure to integrate labor market, organizational, and individual variables; and insufficient conceptual development of turnover-process models to guide research design and interpretation. Thus the manager or personnel researcher must carefully assess the causes and correlates of turnover in the organization(s) to be studied. The research summarized in this chapter should facilitate identifying *potentially* relevant variables. In Chapter 6 we evaluate several integrative models of turnover causes and correlates.

A simplified model of turnover determinants is presented in Fig. 5.1. The term "determinants" is used here in a generic sense to describe any variable potentially related to turnover — either

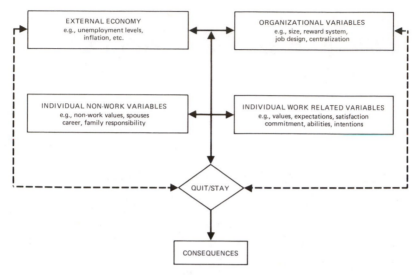

Fig. 5.1. *A simplified model of the causes and correlates of turnover.*

directly, indirectly, causally, or correlationally. The general classes of determinants of turnover are: the state of the economy (for example, the availability of alternative jobs); organizational variables, such as leadership, reward system, job design, etc.; and individual variables. Note that individual variables are related to turnover in two ways. First, external factors such as a spouse's career, family considerations, and leisure preferences may influence an individual's turnover behavior. Second, the individual's job-related values, expectations and abilities, and the individual's *perceptions* and *evaluations* of the external economy, external job factors, and organizational factors may be directly related to turnover.

Several comments about this general model are in order. Since there are four general classes of determinants, (economy, organizational, individual nonwork- and work-related) focusing on any one of them will lead to an incomplete and perhaps inadequate understanding of turnover. For example, in the mid-1970s an executive of a major textile firm reported, "we have made great strides in improving the job satisfaction of our employees as evidenced by the dramatic reduction in turnover." The potential fallacy in this statement is that even if changes in satisfaction had been measured, changes in the economy and the availability of alternative jobs were being ignored. The executive made this statement in 1974 during a period of economic recession.

The model in Fig. 5.1 also calls to our attention the fact that turnover is ultimately an individual behavior. Thus we must be concerned with how the individual employee perceives and evaluates the economy and various organizational factors, and how (s)he integrates work and external-to-work factors.

Our objective in this chapter is to summarize the available research on the economic, organizational, and individual causes and correlates of turnover. Before proceeding, however, it is necessary to focus on several caveats in the literature on turnover.

SEVERAL CAVEATS IN TURNOVER RESEARCH

The causes and correlates of employee turnover have been studied from many different perspectives. The economist may focus on the relationship between average wages and turnover rates by type of industry (Burton and Parker, 1969; Armknecht and Early, 1972). The human resource planner may look at turnover rates by occupational category, length of service, EEO group, etc. (Walker, 1980). The sociologist may compare such variables as occupational group, work group size, or communication pattern (Price, 1977). The industrial-organizational psychologist may study such individual determinants of turnover as job dissatisfaction (Hulin, 1968), commitment (Mowday, Steers, and Porter, 1979), or behavioral intentions to leave (Kraut, 1975; Mobley, Horner, and Hollingsworth, 1978).

From each of these perspectives a contribution to the understanding of employee turnover has been made; however, several caveats must be carefully noted. Many studies of turnover are based on aggregate or grouped data. Thus the relationships studied are between turnover *rates* and individuals *grouped* by the variables thought to be related to turnover. For example, one could compare turnover rates by level of unemployment in the economy, by occupational group, by average job satisfaction within departments, and so forth. For some purposes, this grouped-level analysis can be useful. In human resource planning, analyzing such aggregate relationships may permit forecasting of turnover rates among the various grouping variables. For example, knowing that turnover, on the average, is higher among younger employees, or that it is highest in departments with the most job dissatisfaction, may be useful in projecting the number of quits in certain groups and the number of required replacements. However, it is important to note that such aggregate or grouped analysis does *not* permit prediction or understanding of which *individuals* will leave or stay. Such prediction requires individual rather than grouped analyses.

Another caveat is that many studies of turnover focus on only one or two variables, but analyzed individually. A number of the probable causes and correlates of turnover are interrelated. Thus individual analysis precludes any statement of *relative importance* within a set of variables. Studies which concurrently assess multiple determinants of turnover, such as multivariate analyses, are particularly useful but until recently have been infrequent.

Yet another caveat is that some studies of turnover are retrospective; that is, they seek the causes of turnover after it has occurred. For example, exit interviews may be used in an attempt to get leavers to articulate their reasons for leaving. Exit interviews can be useful sources of diagnostic information (see Lefkowitz and Katz, 1969). However, due to the individual's tendency to rationalize and report selectively, retrospective exit-interview analyses are not substitutes for predictive analyses. With predictive analyses, variables thought to be related to turnover are measured in advance and their relationship to subsequent turnover is assessed. In further discussions, we recommend predictive rather than retrospective analyses.

A final caveat concerns the measurement of change and its relationship to turnover. The four primary classes of determinants of turnover are each in a constant state of change. Thus in our analysis of the determinants of turnover we need to isolate this change and relate it to turnover. Surprisingly few studies have attempted to focus on the dynamic nature of the turnover process via longitudinal analyses (see Porter, Crampon, and Smith, 1976; Graen and Ginsburgh, 1977; and Youngblood, Laughlin, Mobley, and Meglino, 1980, for notable exceptions). Even fewer studies have used a field experimental design to show that changes in potential determinants can result in changes in turnover (see Hulin, 1968; Horner, Mobley, and Meglino, 1979; Wanous, 1973, for further exceptions). We will discuss the dynamic nature of the turnover process more later.

One trait the reader may acquire here is a healthy skepticism when reading studies of employee turnover in internal reports, research journals, professional magazines, or elsewhere. Table 5.1 provides a partial list of questions one might ask when reading and evaluating reports on turnover research.

TABLE 5.1
Some critical questions when evaluating studies of the determinants of employee turnover

---

1. Is this an individual or group level of analysis?

2. Are the interpretations and conclusions consistent with the level of analysis; that is, if the analysis is based on groups, is the author inappropriately giving individual-level interpretations?

3. Are multiple possible determinants of turnover evaluated in such a way as to provide estimates of the relative importance of the determinants (preferred) or are variables studied one at a time?

4. Since no single study can measure all possible determinants, are major alternative explanations of the results logically evaluated?

5. Is the study predictive (preferred) or retrospective?

6. Does the study attempt to capture the dynamic nature of the turnover process; that is, has an attempt been made to deal with relationships between turnover and *changes* in the labor market, organization and individual?

RESEARCH ON THE DETERMINANTS OF TURNOVER

In this century we have seen a steadily increasing flow of research on turnover. Steers and Mowday (1981) report over 1000 studies of turnover in this century. As the second half of the century evolved, sufficient research had been reported to permit several reviews of the literature. Brayfield and Crockett (1955) and Vroom (1964) furnished useful critiques of the literature.

Also during this period, March and Simon (1958) presented their influential conceptual model dealing with the employee's decision to participate in or leave the organization and Vroom (1964) presented his expectancy model of employee choice behavior. We will discuss these and other conceptual models in the next chapter.

In the last quarter of this century, additional research and conceptual developments stimulated several additional reviews, such as Goodman, Salipante, and Paransky (1973) on hardcore unemployment and retention, and Pettman (1973) on the March and Simon (1958) model. More extensive reviews were published by Porter and Steers, 1973; Locke, 1976; Forrest, Cummings, and Johnson, 1977; Price, 1977; Muchinsky and Tuttle, 1979; Hinrichs, 1980; and Mobley, Griffeth, Hand, and Meglino, 1979. These reviews are characterized by their recognition of the multiple determinants of turnover and of the need for integrative conceptual models for better understanding of the turnover process.

In the sections that follow, we discuss existing research. Rather than list each study we summarize and, where possible, suggest generalizations. The reviews of Mobley *et al.* (1979), Muchinsky and Tuttle (1979), Porter and Steers (1973) and Price (1977) are particularly useful and we encourage the reader to refer to them. Specific studies are discussed in detail only when they are particularly illustrative. Although the various determinants of turnover are interrelated, for clarity of discussion we will discuss each of the general classes of determinants suggested in Fig. 5.1 (economic, organizational, and individual). We will then discuss a number of integrative concepts and multivariate studies.

THE EXTERNAL ECONOMY

The state of the economy can be indexed in a variety of ways, including unemployment and employment levels, job vacancy rates, gross national product, balance of trade, rate of inflation, etc. Of particular interest in the study of turnover are economic indices related to supply and demand in the labor market. In this section, relationships between employment-unemployment and turnover rates are examined. In addition, possible effects on turnover rates of projected changes in the composition and mix of the labor force are discussed.

Employment-unemployment Levels

An apparent relationship exists between turnover rates and the state of the economy as indexed by employment-unemployment levels. March and Simon (1958, p. 100) suggested that "under nearly all conditions, the most accurate single predictor of labor turnover is the state of the economy," (as indexed by the availability of jobs). Price (1977), in reviewing the literature on employment levels and turnover rates, found no evidence to contradict this relationship.

Figure 5.2 illustrates this relationship by plotting the average monthly manufacturing quit rate and annual percentage of the labor force unemployed 1969–1979 (BLS, January 1980). As unemployment goes up, the quit rate goes down and vice versa, as evidenced in this figure. Hulin (1979) recently reported a correlation of −0.84 between unemployment and quits across thirty-one years.

It is important to recognize that the relationships discussed above are aggregate. From a managerial perspective, the organization should assess the relationship between employment-unemployment in its specific labor markets and turnover among its employees. Further, overall unemployment as a predictor fails to account for occupational differences in labor market demand. For example, even though unemployment in 1980 was above 7 percent, certain occupations such as computer programming, nursing, and skilled crafts are in demand; as a group they would

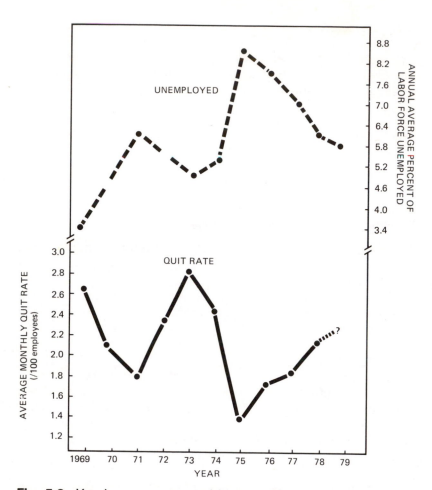

Fig. 5.2. *Yearly average monthly manufacturing quit rate and annual average percent of labor force unemployed, 1969–1979.*
Source: U.S. Department of Labor, Bureau of Labor Statistics, January, 1980.*

---

*The Department of Labor's Bureau of Labor Statistics defines "quits" as terminations of employment initiated by the employee, failure to report after being hired, and unauthorized absences, if on the last day of the month the person has been absent more than seven consecutive calendar days. Rates are expressed per 100 employees. See DOL-BLS, January, 1980, p. 222 for further explanation.

be expected to exhibit higher turnover rates than occupations in low demand.

For human resource planning purposes within the organization, breaking down the relationship between turnover and employment-unemployment into specific geographic labor markets and occupational groupings should enhance the usefulness of the relationship between turnover and indices of the state of the economy. We will discuss techniques for accomplishing this later in the chapter.

Aggregate analyses of economic and labor market correlates of turnover rates, whether for the total labor market or categorized by industry, occupation, region, etc., do not address the question of which *individuals* will leave. Effective understanding and management of turnover requires the analysis of individual-level variables. Such analysis requires individual employee perceptions of the availability of acceptable alternative jobs or surrogate unobtrusive indices of individuals' perceptions of the labor market. We will discuss this issue further in the section on individual determinants of turnover.

Labor-Force Composition and Mix

The remainder of the twentieth century will be characterized by a significantly different labor-force composition and mix relative to the preceding decades. We are currently in a "baby-bust" rather than "baby-boom" period and the population is aging due to the earlier baby boom. While economists are actively analyzing the implications of these changes, the management and human resource literature have not focused on the scope and implications of these changes. Drucker (1980) suggests that an important development in the coming decade is the changing structure and dynamics of the labor force. Turnover is certainly one important implication of the changing labor-force composition and mix.

Wharton Economic Forecasting Associates (Wachter and Kim, 1979) provides a useful analysis of the changing composition of the population and labor forces. Their findings include: between the late 1950s and the late 1970s, the fertility rate dropped from 3.8 to 1.8 children per family, and annual births dropped from 4 to 3.1 million; relatedly, the age distribution of the U.S. population is imbalanced, with a relatively smaller group under 16 years of age and a relatively large 25–44 year-old age group reflecting the recent baby bust and the earlier baby boom respectively; between 1980 and 1995, the number of young people will decline approximately 25 percent, a decline both in percentage and absolute numbers unprecedented in the history of the United States; the decline in the number of young people in the labor force is likely to be even sharper than the population decline since school enrollment rates are projected to begin rising again and labor-force participation rates for younger females are projected to stabilize around 53 percent by 1985 after exhibiting dramatic increases during the 1970s (Wachter and Kim, 1979).

The factors discussed above are likely to lead to a highly competitive and expensive labor market for younger employees in the coming decade and in subsequent decades.

Possible effects of this changing labor market on employee turnover include: more movement of younger employees to other organizations, resulting in higher predicted turnover; greater costs in replacing employees who quit; more emphasis placed on training, since favorable selection ratios will be less prevalent in this cohort of the labor market; and, as we discussed in Chapter 4, organizations may have to expand their efforts to increase labor-force participation among younger people through, for example, using more part-time employees, students, and flexible hours (Nollen, 1980).

As the relatively large post-World War II baby-boom cohort ages and moves through mid-career during the 1980s, organizations will be challenged to provide meaningful careers, training and development, and work assignments (Walker, 1980). To the extent that career aspirations of the baby-boom cohort are not being met, and assuming the availability of alternative jobs, increased turnover may be expected (Schein, 1978).

In addition to the changing age composition of the labor force, changes in occupational distributions may be expected. Table 5.2 presents the percentage distribution of employment by

TABLE 5.2

Relative employment by occupation 1985 projections

PERCENTAGES

Occupational Group	1970	1985 BLS Occupational Demand Model	1985 Labor Supply Model
Professional and technical workers	14.836	15.097	15.498
Managers and administrators except farm	8.322	10.806	7.577
Sales workers	7.123	6.208	6.974
Clerical workers	17.959	10.204	19.654
Craft and kindred workers	13.868	13.141	12.806
Operatives	17.539	14.962	17.498
Nonfarm laborers	4.492	4.610	4.278
Service workers	12.762	14.190	13.079
Farmers and farm laborers	3.085	1.782	2.675
Total	100.000	100.000	100.000

Source: Wachter, Michael L, (1980). The labor market mechanism and immigration: The outlook for the 1980's. *Industrial and Labor Relations Review* **3**: 347. Reprinted with permission from *The Industrial and Labor Relations Review,* Cornell University. All rights reserved.

occupational group for 1970 and the projected supply and demand for these same occupational groups in 1985 (See Wachter, 1980 for details of the methodology).

Inspection of the 1985 projections reveals several interesting points. Demand may exceed supply for managers and administrators, craft and kindred workers, nonfarm laborers, and service workers.

Inflation

Few empirical researchers have addressed the possible relationship between inflation and turnover. Inflation can influence turnover and other turnover-related variables in a number of ways, including: (1) encouraging more secondary wage earners to enter the labor market to supplement family earnings; (2) encouraging turnover as a means to protect earnings, assuming higher-paying jobs are available; (3) discouraging turnover involving geographic mobility due to the cost of moving. Given the high rate of inflation in recent years, greater research emphasis on the relationship between inflation and turnover at both the aggregate and individual levels would be useful.

Summary of Economic Variables

There is ample evidence of a strong negative aggregate relationship between unemployment levels and turnover rates. However, unemployment is unevenly distributed across geographic regions, industries, or occupations. From a managerial perspective this relationship should be disaggregated to compare the organization's turnover with appropriate labor markets. Inflation may influence turnover but this relationship has been inadequately researched. The dramatic change in the composition of the labor force will have significant effects on management in general (Drucker, 1980) and certainly on turnover. From the individual perspective, it is necessary to assess how individuals perceive the availability of alternative jobs.

ORGANIZATIONAL VARIABLES

In this section we summarize the sizable literature on relationships between organizational variables and turnover. The focus here is on categorical, structural, and descriptive characteristics of organizations and the relationships discussed are aggregate. Satisfaction with various organizational variables and other attitudinal variables are discussed in the section on individual determinants.

Type of Industry

There is evidence of interindustry variation in turnover rates. However, because industry rates are infrequently cross-tabulated with occupation, size, geography, or other potentially relevant variables, strong generalizations are not possible.

The BNA-ASPA analyses reported in Table 1.1 reveal that for 1978–80, the finance and health-care industries exhibited the highest total separation rates, while manufacturing exhibited the lowest rates. Price (1977) classifies turnover rates by type of organization for 53 studies from 1947–1971. He found that manufacturing had the highest median separation rate and that goods-producing organizations had over twice the separation rate of service-producing organizations. A comparison of Price's conclusions and the more recent BNA-ASPA data is difficult because of differences in time period, criteria, and sample composition. It is important to note that in both the BNA and Price analyses, there is a large *range* of turnover within a category. This variance suggests that there are strong influences on turnover other than the type of industry.

From a descriptive perspective, a manager might want to compare his/her organization's turnover rate with the rate for the relevant type of industry. BNA (1980), Bureau of Labor Statistics, and trade association reports are useful for this type of bench mark comparison. As an example, Table 5.3 reports the 1979 quit rate by type of industry (Bureau of Labor Statistics, 1980). How-

TABLE 5.3
Labor turnover rates in manufacturing by major industry group.

MAJOR INDUSTRY GROUP	TOTAL			QUITS			LAYOFFS		
	Jan. 1979	Dec. 1979	Jan. 1980	Jan. 1979	Dec. 1979	Jan. 1980	Jan. 1979	Dec. 1979	Jan. 1980
Manufacturing	3.8	3.5	4.1	1.8	1.1	1.6	1.1	1.7	1.6
Seasonally adjusted	4.1	4.0	4.2	2.3	1.9	2.0	.9	1.2	1.3
Durable goods	3.5	3.2	3.9	1.6	.9	1.4	.9	1.6	1.6
Lumber and wood products	5.9	6.0	6.0	3.0	1.8	2.6	1.8	3.3	2.6
Furniture and fixtures	5.2	3.5	5.0	3.3	1.6	2.5	.8	1.2	1.4
Stone, clay, and glass products	4.9	4.8	5.0	1.7	1.1	1.4	2.3	3.0	2.7
Primary metal industries	2.5	3.3	3.2	.9	.5	.7	.6	2.0	1.6
Fabricated metal products	3.9	3.4	4.4	1.8	1.1	1.6	1.1	1.6	2.0
Machinery, except electrical	2.5	1.9	2.7	1.3	.7	1.2	.4	.6	.7
Electric and electronic equipment	3.2	2.2	3.3	1.5	.9	1.4	.7	.6	1.0
Transportation equipment	3.2	3.5	...	1.1	.5	...	1.1	2.4	...

Instruments and related products	2.5	1.9	2.7	1.4	.9	1.6	.3	.5	.4
Miscellaneous manufacturing	5.8	6.5	6.3	2.5	1.4	2.1	2.1	4.4	3.3
Nondurable goods	4.3	4.0	4.4	2.1	1.4	2.0	1.3	1.9	1.6
Food and kindred products	5.9	6.1	6.0	2.6	2.0	2.4	2.4	3.4	2.6
Tobacco manufacturers	5.3	3.0	...	.7	.5	...	3.6	1.9	...
Textile mill products	4.5	3.4	4.6	2.7	1.6	2.6	.8	1.1	.9
Apparel and other products	6.0	5.4	5.9	3.0	1.8	3.0	2.2	3.0	2.2
Paper and allied products	2.7	2.6	2.8	1.2	.7	1.0	.8	1.3	1.0
Printing and publishing	3.4	2.9	3.3	1.9	1.6	1.8	.8	.7	.8
Chemicals and allied products	1.7	1.3	1.7	.7	.5	.7	.4	.4	.4
Petroleum and coal products	2.0	2.1	2.3	.7	.5	.7	.5	1.2	.6
Rubber and miscellaneous plastic products	4.4	4.4	5.2	2.4	1.6	1.9	.9	2.1	2.2
Leather and leather products	6.5	5.9	7.4	3.7	2.4	3.2	1.8	2.8	3.1

Source: U.S. Department of Labor, Bureau of Labor Statistics, *Monthly Labor Review,* April 1980, p. 80.

ever, such data do not provide diagnostic information regarding *who* is leaving — good or poor performers — and *why* they are leaving, e.g., pay, job content, etc. Such additional information is important if turnover is to be understood and effectively managed.

Occupational Categories

Since the nature and technology of an organization may dictate the use of differing occupational categories, it is potentially helpful to assess the relationship between occupational groupings and turnover rates. Price (1977) presents an integration of the published literature on turnover by occupational group. He concludes that there is some support for the generalizations that turnover is higher: (1) among blue-collar workers than white-collar workers; (2) lower skill levels within blue collar; and (3) nonmanagerial categories. He notes the need to qualify these generalizations, due to a paucity of data and/or concern for sampling.

A manager may find it useful to compare turnover rates by occupational group within his/her organization to those in the industry and relevant labor market. The more detailed the occupational breakdown is, the more useful the analysis for diagnosis and forecasting will be.

Organizational Size

Conceptually, we can argue that organizational size is associated with lower turnover, since larger organizations might have more internal mobility opportunities, sophisticated personnel selection and human resource management processes, more competitive compensation systems, and personnel research activities devoted to turnover. However, we can also argue that larger organizations will experience higher turnover due to communication problems, lower group cohesion, and greater impersonalization and bureaucratization. Empirically, the research on turnover and organizational size supports no clear-cut conclusion (Mobley *et al.,* 1979; Porter and Steers, 1973; Price, 1977). BNA (1980) reports that in its sample, organizations with less than 250 employees had the highest average monthly turnover (total separations less temporary and indefinite layoffs) in 1979 (2.2 percent) while organizations with 2500 or more employees had the lowest (1.3 percent). If organizational size does influence turnover, it is indirect through the effects of other variables.

Work-Unit Size

Work-unit size is also possibly related to turnover through other variables like group cohesion, personalization, and communications. There is some evidence that smaller work units, particularly at the blue-collar level, have lower turnover (Muchinsky and Tuttle, 1979; Porter and Lawler, 1965; Porter and Steers, 1973). However, because there are relatively few studies analyzing unit size, either singularly or in combination with other possible explanatory variables, a strong generalization is not possible.

Pay

Researchers have established that there is a strong relationship between pay levels and turnover rates. In a detailed analysis of manufacturing quit rates, Armknecht and Early (1972) found that the most important factor determining interindustry variations in voluntary separations is the relative level of earnings. Turnover is highest in low-paying industries. In addition, they noted a steady progression in the importance of earnings as an explanation for interindustry variations in quits from 1960–1971. A slight decline in the relative importance of earnings was noted in times of business-cycle down-swings and was attributed to a shift in emphasis from wage betterment to job security. Other studies have reached similar conclusions about the aggregate-level relationship between pay levels and turnover rates (see Blau, 1973; Fry, 1973; Price, 1977).

The aggregate correlation between pay levels and turnover rates does not in itself indicate that leavers migrate to higher-paying jobs. However, there is evidence that this is the case. Hellriegel and White (1973) found that CPAs who quit reported 20 percent higher earnings on their new jobs. Wertheimer (1970) and Dalton and Todor (1979) argue that mobility results in net positive income to the migrators. This conclusion, combined with high inflation rates and voluntary or mandatory wage-increase suppression, could contribute to higher turnover rates in the 1980s as individuals seek higher-paying positions.

Although there is ample evidence of the aggregate relationship between pay levels and turnover rates, we must keep several factors in mind. As with other aggregate relationships, it does not allow us to predict or adequately understand individual turnover. Aggregate analysis of pay levels and turnover ignores the important issues of equity in pay administration, individual differences in the importance of pay, and the effects of performance-contingent or noncontingent pay systems (Lawler, 1973). Further, we have an insufficient understanding of the substitutability for pay or interaction of pay with: other organizational factors such as supervisory style and job content; nonjob factors such as compatibility with nonwork roles; and individual factors such as willingness to defer immediate gratification or rewards, commitment, etc.

Job Content

In the last decade we have seen a dramatic increase in interest in job design. This topic receives considerable attention in the subsequent section on individual variables since it is thought that behavioral and attitudinal responses to the job are heavily dependent on individual differences. In this section we focus on the aggregate relationship between turnover and certain job characteristics, including routinization or task repetitiveness, job autonomy and responsibility. Price (1977) indicates that there is a weak but consistent positive relationship between routinization and turnover. Porter and Steers (1973) found support for a positive relationship between task repetitiveness and turnover and a negative relationship between autonomy, responsibility, and turnover. However, we should heed Hulin and Blood (1968) and others who have persuasively argued that workers' responses to job content are a function of individual differences.

Supervisory Style

In theory, we can describe supervisory behavior style independently of the employee's evaluation or reaction to that style. Several studies have explored the aggregate relationship between supervisory consideration (people orientation) and supervisory initiating structure (task orientation). One study found that turnover was highest in work groups whose foreperson was inconsiderate, regardless of the degree of structure (Fleishman and Harris, 1962; Skinner, 1969). However, this relationship is curvilinear; that is, there are critical levels beyond which there is no further effect on turnover rates. Ley (1966) found a strong correlation between foreperson authoritarianism and turnover among production workers. Saleh, Lee, and Prien (1965) found that the lack of supervisory consideration is the second most frequently cited reason for termination among nurses.

Some support for the relationship between supervisory style and turnover is apparent. We will discuss the more frequently studied relationship between satisfaction with supervision and turnover in the section on individual variables.

Other Organizational Variables

Price (1977) suggests that centralization (the degree to which power is centralized in a social system) produces higher levels of turnover; integration (the extent of participation in primary relationships), and communications (the degree to which information is transmitted among members of a social system) produce lower levels of voluntary turnover. He argues that there is strong evidence to support these propositions (p. 67). However, the relative importance of these variables has not been adequately researched. Price (1977) recognizes that relationships between centralization, integration, communications, and turnover are based on the assumption that individuals value participation in decision making and in groups, and receipt of information. We will deal with these assumptions in the section on individual-level variables.

Summary of Organizational Variables

The only strong generalization that can be made regarding aggregate analyses of organizational variables is that turnover rates are higher in lower-paying industries. However, there is some evidence that larger work-group size and lower skill levels among blue-collar workers are associated with higher turnover rates; and that routinization or task repetitiveness, low supervisory consideration, high centralization, low integration, and low communication are associated with higher turnover rates.

INDIVIDUAL VARIABLES

We now turn from the description and analysis of economic and organizational variables to the analysis of individual-level correlates of turnover. Such analysis involves individual demographic and personal factors, work and nonwork values, and perceptions and evaluations of the external economy and the organization. In this section, we will summarize the voluminous literature on individual variables and turnover as an aid in formulating hypotheses regarding the causes and correlates of turnover within an organization.

Demographic and Personal Factors

Age.   Reviewers of the turnover literature report a consistent negative relationship between age and tenure — younger employees have a higher probability of leaving (Mobley *et al.,* 1979; Muchinsky and Tuttle, 1979; Porter and Steers, 1973; Price, 1977). The age-turnover relationship may be based on a number of influences. Younger employees may have more entry-level job opportunities and few family responsibilities, thus making job mobility easier. They may also have inaccurate expectations regarding working which are not fulfilled in their early jobs (Porter and Steers, 1973; Wanous, 1980). We pay particular attention to younger employees in the chapter on managing turnover.

Tenure.   As with age, reviewers of the turnover literature report a consistent negative relationship between length of service and turnover. Turnover is significantly higher for shorter-tenure employees. Mangione (1973), in a national multivariate study, found that length of service is one of the best predictors of turnover.

The U.S. Civil Service Commission (1977) found that in any given cohort of hires, two-thirds to three-fourths of the quits will occur by the end of the first three years of service; of these, more than half will occur by the end of the first year alone. This relationship is shown in Fig. 5.3.

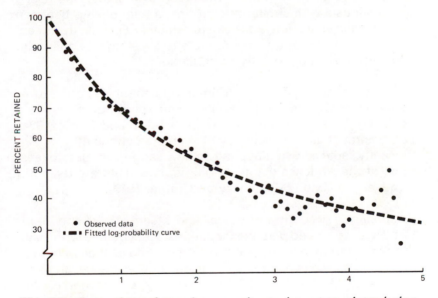

Fig. 5.3. *Retention of employee cohorts by years since being hired.*

Source: U.S. Civil Service Commission, 1977.

The point we emphasize here is that turnover is relatively high in the early years of employment. Interaction with age, inadequate match between job and individual, and inadequate early socialization (Horner *et al.,* 1979; Wanous, 1980; Schein, 1978) are among the probable reasons for this relationship. We focus on early turnover in the chapter on managing turnover.

Sex. No simple pattern emerges when we examine the litera-ture on the relationship between the sex of the employee and turnover (Mobley, *et al.,* 1979; Price, 1977). Sex probably inter-acts with other variables as does occupation and family responsibility.

Education. Neither a strong nor a consistent relationship be-tween education and turnover is evident in the literature (Mobley, *et al.,* 1979; Price, 1977). Since many turnover studies are based on individuals with similar educations, a relationship between turnover and education is difficult to establish. Further, the mean-ingfulness of education as a variable is questionable given the wide disparity in the quality of education.

Biographical data. The development of situation-specific turn-over prediction, based on weighted biographical data, can be a useful empirical technique. Although Schwab and Oliver (1974) demonstrate that the adequacy of such predictions may be sig-nificantly reduced when applied to new samples of employees, most of the evidence suggests biographical data are useful in turnover prediction (Muchinsky and Tuttle, 1979).

Personality. According to Porter and Steers (1973), the litera-ture on turnover and personality suggests that people who leave the organization tend to be at the extreme end of such personal-ity factors as achievement, aggression, independence, and self-confidence. Muchinsky and Tuttle (1979) suggest that personality differences have a marginal impact on turnover (p. 48). Given the probable interaction between personality and organizational environment and given the relatively poor record of personality measures in predicting job behaviors, the lack of a stronger relationship with turnover is not surprising.

Interests. Porter and Steers (1973) and Muchinsky and Tuttle (1979) reviewed the literature relating turnover and vocational interests. Both reviews conclude that the more similar job requirements and vocational interests are, the lower the turnover rate is. However, the amount and quality of research on this relationship is limited.

Aptitude and ability. There is evidence in the literature that aptitude and ability measures (as well as general intelligence measures) are related to turnover. The problem is that the nature and magnitude of the reported relationships vary (Muchinsky and Tuttle, 1979). We suggest that organizations *do* try to use job-relevant aptitude and ability measures as predictors of turnover. Care should be exercised in exploring and documenting the relationship. Further, we should recognize that selection alone will be an insufficient basis for managing turnover.

Source of referral. Several studies have shown that the source of new employee referral is associated with turnover (Gannon, 1971; Reid, 1972; Decker and Cornelius, 1979). According to these studies, applicants referred by informal sources such as employees or relatives, may have lower turnover than applicants referred by more formal sources such as employment agencies and advertising. Although the relationship between the source of referral and turnover has been infrequently evaluated in the research literature, the results are sufficient proof for us to recommend that managers evaluate referral sources.

From a conceptual perspective, the relationship between the source of referral and turnover requires further explanation. It is possible that applicants from the informal sources have more accurate information and expectations about the job (Decker and Cornelius, 1979; Wanous, 1980). '

Professionalism. After reviewing the literature on professionalism and turnover, Price (1977) concluded that there is little support for the notion that successively higher amounts of professionalism are associated with higher levels of turnover.

Bartol (1979) recently analyzed the relationship between the dimensions of professionalism, professional reward criteria, turnover expectations (for stayers), and turnover. She found that professionalism in total, professional commitment in particular, and professionalism plus professional reward criteria are negatively related to turnover expectancy among those who remained with the organization. Although professionalism did not explain a significant amount of variance in turnover, the perceived use of professional reward criteria was significantly and negatively related to turnover; that is, the more the use of professional reward criteria was perceived, the lower the turnover was.

This study suggests that professionalism alone is not a direct determinant of turnover. Rather, perceived professional reward criteria are the most salient variables. We will discuss reward criteria more fully in the chapter on turnover management. Combining Price's (1977) review and the more recent literature cited above leads us to generalize that the relationship between professionalism and turnover is inconclusive.

Performance. The relationship between turnover and the performance of the employee is extremely important. From both determinant and consequence perspectives, it is necessary to evaluate the individual performance-turnover relationship. Surprisingly few researchers have examined this relationship at length (Porter and Steers, 1973; Price, 1977, Martin, 1981). A number of the existing studies purporting to evaluate this relationship did not use actual performance criteria; many studies were conducted in academic institutions; and the pattern of results was mixed (Martin, Price, and Mueller, 1981). For example, Bassett (1967) found that improving performers were more likely to leave; Seybolt, Pavett, and Walker (1978) found higher performers were less likely to leave; and Martin *et al.* (1981) found no relationship between performance and turnover. Thus the performance-turnover relationship is best characterized as inconclusive. It is clear that more research is needed in this area. From a managerial perspective, the performance of stayers and leavers is an important piece of information needed to analyze and effectively manage turnover and will be emphasized in subsequent chapters.

Absenteeism. Turnover and absenteeism are frequently considered part of the same withdrawal process. However, the research evidence is inconclusive. A major oil company, in a proprietary internal report, found an individual-level correlation of .22 between absenteeism during the previous year and turnover. Mirvis and Lawler (1977), on the other hand, found no relationship between absenteeism and turnover among bank employees. Whether absenteeism is best thought of as a precursor of turnover, as an alternative form of withdrawal, or as having no consistent relationship to turnover (Burke and Wilcox, 1972) remains to be determined. Porter and Steers (1973) suggest that, "too often in the past absenteeism has been considered simply an analogue of turnover, and it has been assumed without sufficient evidence that the two shared identical roots" (p. 173). They point out that relative to turnover, absenteeism usually has less negative consequences for the individual, is a more spontaneous and easier decision, and may be a substitute for turnover when turnover is precluded. Further, one might expect higher absences among individuals who are actively searching for another job (Gaudet, 1960).

Although the absenteeism-turnover relationship is inconclusive, the organization may want to track this relationship over time to assess whether absenteeism has diagnostic and predictive value in the organization.

Summary of demographic and personal variables. The only strong conclusions we can draw from this set of variables are that age and tenure are consistently and negatively associated with turnover. There is evidence that weighted biographical information can be useful but must be cross-validated. Further, the limited amount of research on the source of referral suggests a useful relationship, with informal sources exhibiting lower turnover. There is, however, insufficient research to support a strong generalization. Interests, aptitude, and abilities have been related to turnover, but the amount, quality, and results of such research are insufficient to verify these relationships. Finally, the evidence with respect to turnover and personality, sex, education, professionalism, performance, and absenteeism remains inconclusive.

Integrative Variables

A number of variables have been suggested which attempt to integrate individual differences, perceptions of various aspects of the organization, and/or of the external environment. These variables include job satisfaction, career aspirations and expectations, organizational commitment, stress, expectancies regarding alternative jobs, and behavioral intentions. We will summarize the conceptual and empirical evidence of each in relation to turnover.

Job satisfaction.   Satisfaction is a compelling variable. It can be conceptualized as the discrepancy between what an individual values and what the situation provides (Locke, 1976). Thus defined, satisfaction includes both individual differences in values and individual perceptions of organizational variables. One behavioral reaction to dissatisfaction is to withdraw; the reaction to satisfaction, however, is to approach (Locke, 1976).

Overall job satisfaction.   There is undoubtedly a consistent negative relationship between job satisfaction and turnover. Reviews by Brayfield and Crockett (1955), Price (1977), Vroom (1964), Porter and Steers (1973), Locke (1975); Mobley, *et al.* (1979) and Muchinsky and Tuttle (1979) conclude that the literature clearly shows that the lower the job satisfaction is, the greater the probability of turnover is. Although this relationship is consistent, the correlations are rarely stronger than −0.4. Thus we need to use variables other than job satisfaction to predict individual-level turnover. At a minimum, perceived alternative jobs must also be considered (March and Simon, 1958; Forrest, *et al.*, 1977; Mobley, 1977; Mobley, *et al.*, 1978, 1979). In addition, the use of overall satisfaction offers little diagnostic value regarding what aspects of the job are contributing to turnover.

Satisfaction with pay. Porter and Steers' review of the literature reveals a generally consistent negative relationship between turnover and pay satisfaction. The Mobley, *et al.* (1979) review found enough exceptions to advise against taking this relationship as a given in every situation. However, the relationship between pay satisfaction and turnover, combined with the previously discussed aggregate relationship between pay levels and turnover rates, are sufficiently consistent to warrant pay as among the primary hypothesized contributors to turnover in any organizational study.

Satisfaction with promotion. Porter and Steers (1973) indicate that the lack of promotional opportunities is a primary stated reason for withdrawal. The Price (1977) and Mobley, *et al.* (1979) reviews found some support for this relationship but also found exceptions. Without knowing an individual's career aspirations and opportunities for promotion, the predictive power of satisfaction with promotion may be diminished. As we will discuss later, career expectations may interact with current satisfaction in influencing turnover.

Satisfaction with job content. There is an increasing body of evidence that evaluation and satisfaction with job content are consistently and negatively related to turnover (Porter and Steers, 1973; Mobley, *et al.*, 1979). Mobley *et al.* (1979) conclude that satisfaction with job content is among the strongest satisfaction correlates of turnover in recent research. We focus on the issues of job design and job content in the chapter on managing turnover.

Satisfaction with coworkers. There is evidence that the quality of peer-group interactions and satisfaction with coworkers can be related to turnover. However, in a number of studies this relationship was not found at all. Porter and Steers (1973) observe that coworker relationships, like other single dimensions of satisfaction, do not have equivalent degrees of impact on all types of employee groups. It is possible that our measures of coworker relationships and satisfaction are too crude. Coworker relationships have multiple dimensions and reflect task requirements, individual differences, and instrumental and personal relations. For the present, there is only moderate empirical evidence to support the relationship between coworker satisfaction and turnover.

Satisfaction with supervision.   There is also evidence that satisfaction with supervision can be related to turnover, although there are a number of exceptions in the literature. The comments offered in the preceding paragraph apply here as well. Research needs to move beyond general leader-satisfaction ratings to deal with specific leader-subordinate (and peer-group) interactions. In an exemplary research program, Graen and his associates have demonstrated that leader acceptance (that is, the leader's flexibility in changing the employees' job and using his/her power to help employees solve work problems) is significantly related to turnover (Dansereau, Cashman, and Graen, 1974; Graen, 1976; Graen and Ginsburgh, 1977).

Combined with the aggregate supervisory-style research summarized in the section on organizational variables, we can reasonably conclude that supervision is a contributor to employee turnover.

Satisfaction with working conditions.   A number of studies support the theory that turnover is related to various working conditions. In a national survey, Mangione (1973) found a significant relationship between resource adequacy, satisfaction with comfort, and turnover. Except for this study, there is insufficient evidence that working conditions are among the most important contributors to turnover. However, we cannot ignore this set of variables.

Summary of job satisfaction variables.   The research evidence consistently supports the negative relationship between overall satisfaction and turnover. The fact that the correlations are not stronger suggests other variables — such as perceptions of the availability of attractive alternative jobs, relative importance of nonwork values, and career expectations — are also involved in turnover. We will focus on these variables in subsequent sections.

In addition to overall satisfaction, a consistent negative relationship exists between satisfaction with job content and turnover. Less consistent but frequently observed correlations exist between turnover and satisfaction with pay, promotion, supervision, coworkers, and working conditions. Satisfactions, overall and by dimension, are among the integrative variables required for understanding turnover.

From a research perspective, additional studies are required to specify the relative importance of various dimensions of satisfaction in specific settings and how satisfaction relates to other variables in the turnover process.

Career aspirations and expectations.   Job satisfaction is a present-oriented evaluative reaction to one's current job. It may be argued that to completely understand turnover, we must also evaluate the future-oriented reaction — that is, the individual's assessment of whether or not the job will be instrumental in attaining career aspirations (Mobley, *et al.,* 1979). For example, an accountant may be satisfied with his/her job, pay, supervision, and rate of promotion in one of the established CPA firms. However, aspiring to start his/her own CPA firm, the accountant may quit. Conversely, a management trainee may be dissatisfied with the job assignments, rate of promotion, etc. in the training program, but does not quit because (s)he sees the possibility of future assignments. Further, the incidence of major career changes is apparently increasing (Drucker, 1980).

Relatively little research has been devoted to analyzing turnover in terms of congruence between the organization and long-range individual career aspirations. Career aspirations are subject to change, thus this congruence must be considered an ongoing process. The work of Hall (1976), Schein (1978), and others on career development and dynamics represents an area of inquiry that needs to be integrated with the other variables and processes related to turnover.

The chapters on analyzing and managing turnover give considerable attention to relating career and turnover processes.

Organizational commitment.   Organizational commitment has been defined as the relative strength of an individual's identification with and involvement in a particular organization. Further, it has been characterized by at least three factors: (1) a strong belief in and acceptance of the organization's goals and values; (2) a willingness to exert considerable effort on behalf of the organization; and (3) a strong desire to maintain membership in the organization (Mowday, Steers, and Porter, 1979; Steers, 1977; Porter, Crampon, and Smith, 1976).

There is strong evidence that commitment is related to turnover (Porter *et al.,* 1974; Porter *et al.,* 1976; Steers, 1977; Mowday *et al.,* 1979). There is also evidence that commitment is a better predictor of turnover than satisfaction (Porter *et al.,* 1974; Mowday *et al.,* 1979). Conceptually and empirically it is evident that organizational commitment is one of the important individual-level determinants. We will discuss analyzing and developing commitment in later chapters.

Expectancy of finding an alternative job.   The aggregate-level strong negative relationship between unemployment levels and quit rates was reviewed earlier. While unemployment is a good aggregate predictor, it is inadequate at the individual level. Unemployment is not uniformly distributed by region, industry, or occupational grouping. Further, individuals have a differential knowledge of alternatives. From the individual perspective it is important to know the individual employee's expectancy of finding an alternative job.

Several studies have examined employee expectancy of finding an alternative job and found it to be significantly, although not strongly, related to turnover (see Mobley *et al.,* 1978; Mobley, Hand *et al.,* 1979; Miller *et al.,* 1979; Dansereau *et al.,* 1974).

The fact that the correlation between the expectancy of finding an alternative job and turnover is not stronger may be related to: inaccurate or unrealistic expectations if the employee is not actively seeking an alternative job (Mobley *et al.,* 1978); perceptions regarding alternatives are salient only under extreme negative labor market conditions (Miller *et al.,* 1979); individual differences in knowledge of the labor market (March and Simon, 1958); or that this variable influences other variables such as intention to search (Coverdale and Terborg, 1980). However, this variable is sufficiently supported empirically to suggest it is worthy of attention in individual-level analyses of turnover.

Intentions to quit-stay. Conceptually, an individual's behavioral intentions should be a good predictor of behavior (Locke, 1969, 1975, 1976; Fishbein and Ajzen, 1975; Mobley, 1977). Empirically, behavioral intention to quit-stay measures appear to be among the best individual-level predictors of turnover (Kraut, 1975; Miller *et al.,* 1979, Mobley *et al.,* 1978; Newman, 1974; Waters *et al.,* 1976). The periodic assessment of behavioral intentions to quit, and correlates of those intentions, is a turnover forecasting and diagnostic approach we strongly recommend.

Stress. In an enlightening analysis of the literature on stress in organizations, Schuler (1980) defines stress as a dynamic condition in which an individual is confronted with an opportunity, constraint, and/or demand on being/having/doing what (s)he desires and for which the resolution is perceived as uncertain but which will lead to important outcomes (p. 189). Stress may have both positive and negative consequences and may be cumulative in terms of work and nonwork contributing factors.

One of the possible behavioral outcomes of stress is turnover (Schuler, 1980; Van Sell, Brief, and Schuler, 1979). The conceptual and empirical linkages between stress and turnover have been inadequately researched. At present, we must consider this relationship inconclusive. However, given the individual, organizational, and societal importance of stress and its consequences, this relationship deserves more attention.

Individual Nonwork Variables

The relationships between individual nonwork-related variables, economic, organizational, other individual-level variables, and turnover are often neglected. Intuitively, it would appear that an individual's decision to quit a job involves not only an evaluation of the current and possibly future jobs within or outside the organization, but also an evaluation of such nonwork variables as family, leisure preferences, life style, etc.

To date, most turnover research dealing with nonwork variables has focused on what is generally labeled "family responsibility." This is a complex factor that is measured in a variety of ways including the number and ages of children, marital status, etc. Although no simple generalization is possible, Muchinsky and Tuttle (1979) suggest that there is a positive relationship between family responsibility and turnover but it is moderated by whether the employee is the primary or secondary wage earner.

My consulting, research, and personal experiences in the sunbelt over the past decade have led to an increasing sensitization to the importance of nonwork variables. A number of acquaintances have made career decisions involving both quitting a job or not accepting an attractive alternative, to stay in the sunbelt, to not disrupt their children's schooling, or to accommodate a spouse's career.

As dual-career families become more prevalent (Bailyn, 1970; Rapoport and Rapoport, 1976); as nonwork values become more central (Dubin, Champoux, and Porter, 1975); and as more young people attach less importance to a stable and secure career (Schein, 1978), prediction and understanding of turnover will require inclusion of such nonwork variables.

The concept of role conflict is also relevant (Kahn *et al.,* 1964). To the extent that the work role conflicts with other roles, such as parent, coach, or participant in civic or religious activities, etc., one solution is to change work roles.

Although turnover research in this area is sparse, the increasing body of knowledge on career development and career dynamics may well provide the foundation for a better understanding of how turnover relates to the interaction of work and nonwork factors. Schein (1978) provides a useful analysis of the need for managers to consider the "whole person," including one's self, family, and career. We will discuss this further in subsequent chapters.

INTEGRATIVE ANALYSES

As noted earlier, the turnover literature is characterized by studies which look at turnover and one other variable at a time. Such analyses do not permit evaluation of the relationships among the many variables related to turnover, identification of the relative importance of these variables, or the increased prediction of turnover possible when several relevant variables are used. More adequate prediction and understanding of turnover requires using multiple variables in the analysis (Mobley *et al.,* 1979; Price, 1977).

In this section, we summarize integrative or multivariate research and discuss several example studies in detail, first from the aggregate perspective, then from the individual perspective.

Aggregate Analyses

Parsons (1977) provides an integrative review of five economic studies of industry quit rates. Table 5.4 is Parsons' summary of these studies. It is important to note that the magnitude and sign of variables may be influenced by the other variables included in the analyses, and that interpretation must always be qualified by variables not included in a given analysis. Table 5.4 reveals that income has a consistently negative relationship with the quit rate. Further, the product market concentration of the firm is second only to income in terms of strength and consistency of its relationship (negative) to turnover. Parsons suggests that this

TABLE 5.4
Industry quit rates, cross-sectional analyses selected regression
coefficient signs

CHARAC-TERISTICS	STUDIES				
	(1) Stoikov-Raimon	(2) Burton-Parker	(3) Pencavel	(4) Parsons	(5) Telser
A. *Income*	N	N	N**	N**	N**
B. *Skill*					
1. Quality	N	P*	—	P	—
2. Production worker	—	N	—	—	P*
3. Professional worker	—	—	—	P**	—
4. Brief tenure	P**	—	—	P	—
C. *Demographic*					
1. Female	P	P**	P**	N	—
2. Black	N	P**	N	P**	—
3. Youth	—	—	P	—*	—
D. *Industry*					
1. Firm size	N	N	—	—	—
2. Unionization	N*	N	N*	—	—
3. Concentration	—	N**	—	N**	N**
E. *Location rural*	—	P	N*	N	—

N = negative coefficient.   * = significant at α = .05, two-tailed test.
P = positive coefficient.   ** = significant at α = .01, two-tailed test.

Source: D.O. Parsons (1977). Models of labor market turnover: a theoretical and
empirical survey. In R.G. Elrenberg (ed.) *Research in Labor Economics,* JAI
Press. Used with permission.

may reflect the immobilizing effects of reduced competition for industry-specific skills. There is evidence that when income and other variables are held constant, organizations with briefer-tenure employees, a higher percentage of professional and younger workers, and no union, experience higher quit rates. The other variables were relatively inconsistent in sign and/or significance. Parsons (1977) concludes from these analyses that: the quit rate falls when income rises relative to skill levels and rises when quality rises relative to income; and that the demographic and industry characteristics require additional explanation (p. 210).

Individual Analyses

Mangione (1973), in a national survey, used a variety of demographic, satisfaction, and occupational variables to predict turnover. The rank order of the strongest variables was: satisfaction with comfort, satisfaction with coworkers, industry, age, tenure, occupation, satisfaction with financial rewards, occupational prestige, and satisfaction with challenge. It is important to note that demographic, occupational, and satisfaction variables each added to the prediction of turnover. Thus to ignore any one of these classes of variables will lead to a decreased ability to predict and understand turnover.

Mobley, Horner, and Hollingsworth (1978) used intention to quit, intention to search, thinking of quitting, probability of finding an acceptable alternative, satisfaction, and a composite of age and tenure to predict turnover among hospital employees. With the exception of probability of finding an acceptable alternative, each variable individually correlated with turnover. When all the variables were combined, only intention to quit was significantly related to turnover. This result suggests that intentions serve as a summary variable for a number of other correlates of turnover. That is, intentions to quit-stay encompass the effects of a number of other variables that are individually related to turnover.

Miller, Katerberg, and Hulin (1979) evaluated a model using three classes of variables: satisfaction; career mobility (age, ten-

TABLE 5.5
An interpretive summary of research on causes and correlates of turnover

	Consistent	Moderate	Inconclusive
Labor market	Level of unemployment		Inflation
Organizational variables	Pay levels	Supervisory style	Type of industry
		Work-unit size	Organization size
		Routinization, task repetitiveness	
		Autonomy and responsibility	
		Centralization	
		Integration	
		Communication	
Individual variables	Age	Source of referral	Personality
	Tenure	Family responsibility	Sex
	Satisfaction with job content	Interests	Education
		Aptitude and ability	Professionalism
		Satisfaction—pay	Performance
		Satisfaction—promotion	Career expectations
		Satisfaction—coworkers	Absenteeism
		Satisfaction—supervisor	
		Satisfaction—conditions of work	

TABLE 5.5
An interpretive summary of research on causes and correlates of
turnover (continued)

Individual variables		
	Expectancy of finding an alternative	

Integrative variables		
	Overall satisfaction	Stress
	Behavioral intentions to quit	
	Organizational commitment	

ure, probability of finding an acceptable alternative); and withdrawal cognitions (intention to quit, intention to search, thinking
of quitting). Their data were consistent with the interpretation
that satisfaction and career mobility influence turnover through
their influence on withdrawal cognition.

We can draw several conclusions from these and other multivariate studies previously reviewed by Mobley *et al.* (1979).
First, while job satisfaction is an important contributor to turnover, it is not inclusive of the effects of other relevant demographic, attitudinal, or cognitive variables. To predict and
understand individual turnover we must move beyond the simple satisfaction-turnover relationship. Second, demographic
variables are an inadequate basis for understanding turnover.
Third, behavioral intentions to quit or stay appear to be potent
variables, conceptually and empirically. However, the fact that
intentions and turnover are far from perfectly correlated suggests the need for better measurement and to continue to search
for other variables and processes.

SUMMARY

Table 5.5 provides an interpretive summary of research on variables related to turnover. Variables are classified in terms of the support for a strong generalization linking the variable to turnover. The categories "consistent," "moderate," or "inconclusive" are based on the author's evaluation of the quantity, quality, and interpretability of published research. Every variable listed in this table is *potentially* related to turnover. However, the variables listed in the consistent and moderate support columns appear to support the strongest generalizations and thus should receive particular attention in an organizational study. Other variables have been studied but with insufficient frequency to evaluate their relevance. This table is not intended to suggest that the inconclusive variables should be abandoned or that new variables should not be studied. It is important that multiple variables are studied in combination and over time, and that the multiple consequences of turnover (see Chapter 2) are evaluated.

In the next chapter we present models of the turnover process which attempt to conceptually integrate the research summarized in this chapter.

Conceptual Models of Employee Turnover

6

INTRODUCTION

In the preceding chapter we reviewed and summarized the empirical research on the causes and correlates of turnover. A number of variables were shown to be related or potentially related to turnover. Historically, however, a fundamental problem in the turnover literature has been a preoccupation with single relationships and insufficient focus on the conceptual basis of turnover as a psychological process. From both the research and managerial perspectives, it is necessary to have adequate conceptual models of the turnover process to: (1) interpret research findings; (2) suggest new avenues of research; (3) call attention to the multiple determinants of turnover; (4) and to guide managers in diagnosing and dealing with turnover.

Our objective in this chapter is to summarize and critique several conceptual models of the turnover process. As will become evident, the models have common elements, but differ in significant respects. In the summaries and critiques that follow, it is important to remember that a conceptual model cannot be evaluated on a simple correct-incorrect scale. More appropriate criteria include the model's ability to: organize and integrate existing empirical findings; clarify relationships and issues; stimulate new research; and further understanding of the turnover process.

THE MARCH AND SIMON MODEL

One of the earliest and perhaps most influential integrative models of employee turnover was presented by March and Simon (1958) in *Organizations.* The March and Simon "Decision to Participate" model has two distinct, but interrelated, components when applied to employee participation: (a) perceived *desirability of movement* from the organization; and (b) perceived *ease of movement* from the organization.

Figure 6.1 illustrates their concept of the major factors affecting perceived desirability of movement. The two major contributions are job satisfaction and perceived possibility of intraorganizational transfer (p. 93). Job satisfaction is considered a function of conformity of the job to self-image, predictability of job relationships, and compatibility of job and other roles (p. 94–95). Conformity of job to self-image is considered a function

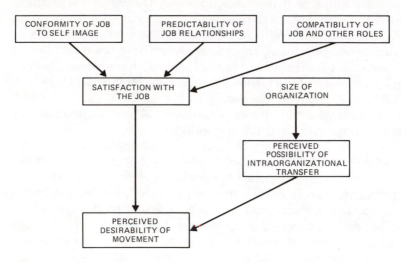

Fig. 6.1. *Major factors affecting perceived desirability of movement.*

Source: J.G. March and H.A. Simon. *Organizations* (New York: Wiley, 1958, p. 99). Copyrighted 1958, Wiley and Sons. Reprinted with permission of publisher and authors.

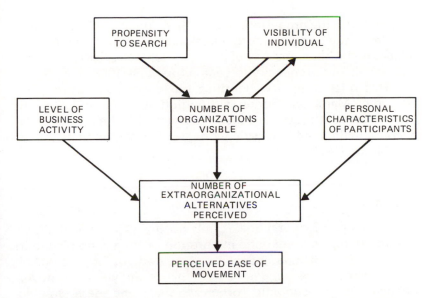

Fig. 6.2. *Major factors affecting perceived ease of movement.*

Source: J.G. March and H.A. Simon. *Organizations* (New York: Wiley, 1958, p. 106). Copyrighted 1958, Wiley and Sons. Reprinted with permission of publisher and authors.

of supervisory practices, amount of rewards, participation in job assignment, education, and rate of change of status and/or income (p. 96–97).

Figure 6.2 illustrates their concept of the major factors affecting perceived ease of movement. "We will hypothesize that perceived ease of movement for an individual depends on the availability of jobs for which he is qualified (and willing to accept) in organizations visible to him" (1958, p. 100). The number of extraorganizational alternatives is considered a function of the level of business activity (pp. 100–101); personal characteristics of participants, including sex, age, social status, tenure and specialization (pp. 101–102); and the number of visible organizations. The latter, at the organizational level, is thought to be related to the prestige, product distinguishability, growth rate, and number of high-status occupations and/or individuals as-

sociated with the organization (p. 103). At the individual participant level, the number of organizations visible is thought to be
related to the heterogeneity of personal contacts, visibility of the
individual, and propensity to search (pp. 103–105).

This brief summary identifies the major hypotheses discussed by March and Simon, although it does not do justice to
the richness of the subhypotheses discussed in their model. We
encourage the reader to review Chapter 4 of the original March
and Simon (1958) book.

Evaluation

The March and Simon model is noteworthy as perhaps the first
one to attempt a systematic integration of the economic-labor
market and individual behavior. A variety of psychological
mechanisms were suggested for linking individual turnover
behavior with economic, organizational, and demographic
variables.

It is both surprising and disappointing that this model has
been subjected to so little empirical research. In presenting the
model, March and Simon cited a great deal of earlier research to
support various hypotheses. While this approach is appropriate
for model and hypothesis generation, it is not a substitute for
subsequent direct evaluation of the model. As noted in the preceding chapter, simple two-variable relationships can be found
between many variables and turnover. However, until these
variables are concurrently evaluated in the context of a conceptual model, the interrelationships and relative contribution of the
set of variables cannot be adequately evaluated.

More recently, Pettman (1973) reviewed the turnover literature from the perspective of the March and Simon model. With
respect to perceived desirability of movement, Pettman concludes that the research evidence consistently supports:

a. job dissatisfaction as a sufficient but not necessary condition for high turnover (p. 43);

b. the hypothesized relationship between predictability of instrumental relationships and satisfaction (p. 43–44);

c. the congruence of work-time patterns and other roles in relation to satisfaction and, consequently, turnover (p. 46);

d. the hypothesis that conformity of the job with respect to self-concept (and the supervisory practices and rate-of-status change components of self-concept) is associated with satisfaction and, subsequently, turnover (pp. 46–48);

e. the hypotheses involving work group size, rewards, education, and perceived possibility of intraorganizational transfer (pp. 47–49).

With respect to perceived ease of movement, Pettman (1973) concludes that there is:

a. reasonable substantiation for the hypothesized relationship between unemployment levels and turnover rates (p. 51);

b. support for the age, length-of-service, and specialization hypotheses (pp. 51–53);

c. equivocal support for the sex and social status hypotheses (p. 50–54).

Thus the literature reviewed by Pettman can be interpreted as consistent with some, but not all, of the hypotheses from the March and Simon model.

In one of the few direct tests of the March and Simon model, Schwab and Dyer (1974) found that turnover is related to desirability of movement as indexed by the satisfaction measures, but not to ease of movement as indexed by the perception of available job opportunities and the degree to which one's personal characteristics facilitate or discourage job change.

Fossum, Keaveny, and Jackson (1977) analyzed willingness to change jobs as a function of both perceived desirability of movement and ease of movement. They found that willingness to change jobs was more strongly related to desirability of movement (dissatisfaction, underutilization of skills, and employment status), than to ease of movement. As noted by the authors, willingness to move is not the same as actual turnover, and only a subset of variables or surrogates were used.

Overall, the March and Simon model has provided a solid foundation for much of the later conceptual work on employee turnover. This model has been a valuable catalyst. Although empirical data consistent with many of the hypotheses can be found, there have been few direct evaluations of the multiple and sequential determinants of turnover suggested by this model. The March and Simon model has contributed to the study of turnover by focusing attention on the need to assess both economic-labor market and behavioral variables in studying the employee turnover process.

THE PRICE MODEL

Price (1977) published an extensive review and codification of the turnover literature. He presented a model of the determinants and intervening variables associated with turnover. Figure 6.3 presents the Price model.

Price defines the primary determinants of turnover as: pay levels; integration (extent of participation in primary or quasi-

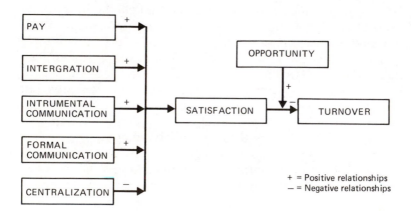

Fig. 6.3. *Price's model of turnover determinants and intervening variables.*

Source: Reprinted by permission from *The Study of Turnover* by James L. Price. Copyrighted 1977 by the Iowa State University Press, Ames, Iowa 50010.

primary relationships); instrumental communication (directly related to role performance); formal communication (officially transmitted); and centralization (degree to which power is centralized) (pp. 68–79). The first four determinants are considered positively related to turnover; the fifth, centralization, negatively related.

The Price model specifies that satisfaction and opportunity are intervening variables between the determinants and turnover. Satisfaction is defined as the degree to which members have a positive attitudinal orientation toward membership in the organization (p. 79). Opportunity is the availability of alternative roles (jobs) in the environment (p. 81).

A fundamental hypothesis of the Price model is that dissatisfaction results in turnover only when opportunity is relatively high, that is, there is an interaction between satisfaction and opportunity (p. 83).

Evaluation

Price makes a positive contribution in attempting to integrate organizational variables such as the determinants, environmental variables such as opportunity, and individual variables such as satisfaction. One criticism of the model from an individual psychological perspective is its lack of specificity regarding how individuals perceive and evaluate the determinants and opportunity. The model must assume that the determinants are equivalently valued outcomes to employees — that individuals have knowledge of alternatives and are unconstrained in pursuing them. These assumptions minimize individual differences in values, and perceptual and evaluative processes. However, Price does specify a number of individual demographic variables, such as age and tenure, that may be correlated with the determinants and intervening variables.

Five empirical tests of the Price model were reviewed by Bluedorn (1980). In all five tests, as well as Bluedorn's results, the hypothesized interaction between satisfaction and opportunity was not found. Further, the effects of the demographic variables were incompletely explained by the model. Bluedorn concludes that these tests support the treatment of opportunity as a predictor of satisfaction rather than as intervening between satisfaction and turnover.

THE MOBLEY INTERMEDIATE LINKAGES MODEL

As noted in the previous chapter, the negative relationship between job satisfaction and turnover is well established, consistent, but usually not particularly strong (Locke, 1975, 1976; Porter and Steers, 1973). Mobley (1977) argues for the need to move beyond simple replication of the satisfaction-turnover relationship toward research on the cognitive and behavioral processes that may occur between satisfaction and actual turnover. Drawing on the conceptual work of March and Simon (1958) and Locke (1975, 1976), Mobley presents a model of the turnover decision process which identifies possible intermediate linkages in the satisfaction-turnover relationship. This model is presented in Fig. 6.4.

This model suggests that dissatisfaction elicits thoughts of quitting, search evaluation and behavior, the evaluation of alternatives, intentions to quit, and ultimately turnover. Feedback loops are suggested at each step of the process. For example, if search for alternatives is unsuccessful, it may lead to reevaluation of the present job and a change in satisfaction. A major hypothesis of this model is that intention to quit is the variable which immediately proceeds turnover. Previous research has demonstrated that intentions to quit are among the strongest predictors of turnover (Porter and Steers, 1973; Mobley et al., 1979).

Evaluation

This model focuses on turnover as a process and questions the role of satisfaction as the immediate precursor of turnover. Research based on simplified versions of the model has generally supported the hypothesis that intentions are the best predictors of turnover and that preceding variables, including satisfaction,

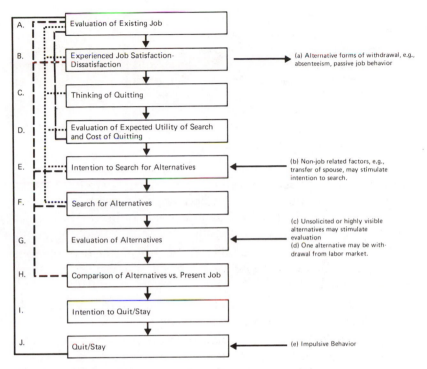

Fig. 6.4. *Mobley's intermediate linkages model.*

Source: W.H. Mobley (1977). Intermediate linkages in the relationship between job satisfaction and employee turnover. *Journal of Applied Psychology* **62**:238. Copyrighted, 1977, American Psychological Association. Reprinted by permission of the publisher and author.

do not add to the prediction of turnover over and above intentions (Coverdale and Terborg, 1980; Miller *et al.*, 1979; Mobley *et al.*, 1978; Mowday *et al.*, 1980).

However, hypothesized internal relationships involving probability of finding an acceptable alternative have been less clear. While probability of finding an acceptable alternative has been shown to be related to thinking of quitting, (Mobley *et al.*, 1978; Coverdale and Terborg, 1980), it has not related to search or intentions as predicted (Miller *et al.*, 1979; Coverdale and Terborg, 1980; Mobley *et al.*, 1978; Mowday *et al.*, 1980).

It is to our benefit to relate the results regarding probability of finding an acceptable alternative in tests of the Mobley model to the results of tests of the previously discussed models. As noted above, the few tests of the March and Simon model have not found strong support for the ease of movement construct. Tests of the Price model have failed to find the hypothesized satisfaction-opportunity interaction.

A number of explanations have been offered for the failure of alternatives to operate as predicated:

1. Once an employee thinks of quitting, his/her intention to search and quit becomes established and persistent, independent of the probability of finding an acceptable alternative (Mobley *et al.*, 1978, p. 413; Coverdale and Terborg, 1980, p. 7).

2. Individuals may not know what alternatives are available until they search. Or individuals may have accurate expectations about alternatives independent of satisfaction and search (Mobley *et al.*, 1978, p. 413; Miller *et al.*, 1979, p. 516).

3. The measurement of the variables may be relatively unreliable, inconsistent, or unstable (Miller *et al.*, 1979, p. 516).

4. An individual's perceptions of the labor market may influence turnover only under extreme negative circumstances (economic recession). Only when there is little chance of finding an alternative do such perceptions constrain negative job attitudes that lead to turnover (Miller *et al.*, 1979, p. 516).

Existing research does not permit evaluation of these alternative explanations. The role of alternatives, ease of movement, and opportunity in the turnover decision process remains to be clearly established.

Although the research to date has been generally supportive of simplified versions of this model, a fundamental issue remains unaddressed. If turnover is to be treated as a process, with appropriate feedback mechanisms as the model suggests, it is necessary to use research designs which trace changes in the many variables over time. As of this writing, no such research on this model has been published. Most research and management reporting on causes of turnover is cross-sectional rather than longitudinal.

THE EXPANDED MOBLEY *ET AL.* MODEL

The last and most detailed model to be discussed is that of Mobley, Griffeth, Hand, and Meglino (1979). This model incorporates elements of the preceding models and attempts to capture the overall complexity of the turnover process. Although it is unlikely that any single study can evaluate this complexity, the authors sought to graphically illustrate the multiple organizational, environmental, and individual variables associated with the turnover process. The expanded Mobley *et al.* model is presented in Fig. 6.5. Since this model is relatively new, we will discuss it in detail.

This model suggests that there are four primary determinants of intentions to quit and subsequently turnover: (1) job satisfaction-dissatisfaction; (2) expected utility of alternative internal (to the organization) work roles; (3) expected utility of external (to the organization) work roles; and (4) nonwork values and contingencies.

Job Satisfaction

We can conceptualize job satisfaction as a present-oriented evaluation of the job involving a comparison of an employee's multiple values and what the employee perceives the job as providing (Locke, 1975, 1976). To the extent that the job is perceived as providing what one highly values, satisfaction is enhanced. To the extent that the job is perceived as not providing what one values, satisfaction is diminished. Several aspects of this conceptualization of job satisfaction are important for understanding both satisfaction and its relationship with turnover.

First, satisfaction is a highly individualized evaluation that is dependent on individual differences in values. Both the magnitude and intensity of what individuals value in the work setting are highly variable. For some individuals, a repetitive job, rotating shifts, no overtime, and congenial coworkers may be valued aspects of a job. For others, involvement in decision making, flexible work hours, and high-incentive earnings may be the most salient work values.

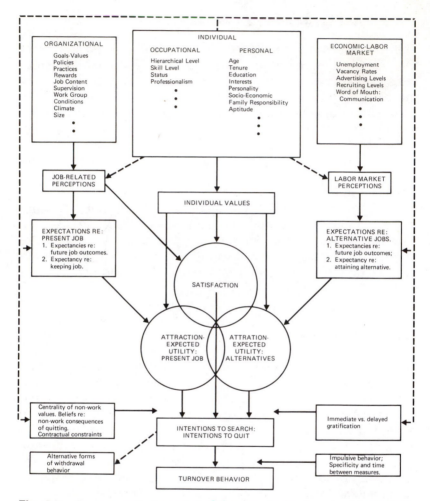

Fig. 6.5. *An expanded model of the employee turnover process.*

Source: W. Mobley, R. Griffeth, H. Hand, and B. Meglino (1979). A review and conceptual analysis of the employee turnover process. *Psychological Bulletin* **86**:517. Copyrighted 1979, American Psychological Association. Reprinted by permission of the publisher and author.

The increasing diversity of work values is a characteristic of the work force which managers must recognize and address. Uniform policies, practices, and procedures, which treat the work force as homogeneous, are likely to be increasingly ineffective because they do not recognize and are not responsive to individual differences in values. Employee selection, assimilation placement, and reward systems must become more sensitive to individual differences in work values.

A second important aspect of this conceptualization of job satisfaction is its emphasis on employee perceptions. Satisfaction is a function of what the employee perceives, that is, what the employee sees or thinks (s)he sees, relative to his/her values. For example, an organization may operate on a performance-based merit pay increase policy — a policy which may be valued by the employee. However, if the employee is unable to *see* this policy in action, due, for example, to highly secretive salary administration (Lawler, 1973), it may contribute to dissatisfaction. Similarly, an employee may value task variety but not perceive its presence, even though management has established a job rotation plan — for example, between box-packing and box-closing. The point is that satisfaction is not a function of formal policy or management perceptions, but of employee perceptions. As discussed earlier, regular assessment of employee perceptions and values is necessary if satisfaction, and its contribution to turnover, is to be understood and effectively managed.

A third aspect of satisfaction is that it is multi-faceted. Since employees have a variety of values, it is unlikely that any one value will control satisfaction unless it is extremely discrepant. Satisfaction is a composite of the extent to which a set of important values are perceived as being attained on the job. Thus an organization that puts all its emphasis on one facet (such as pay, considerate supervision, job content, or working conditions, etc.) may be disappointed. Alternatively, the employer who cannot adequately satisfy one value may be able to partially compensate by enhancing the attainment of other values. For example, the author worked with a midwestern metal fabricating firm which, due to industry cost competition, was unable to be a wage leader in the local labor market. This firm was still able to attract and retain a satisfied and competent work force because job content, working conditions, and management style were responsive to employee values in nonwage areas.

Finally, recall that satisfaction is a present-oriented evaluation of the job. As such, it does not capture the employee's expectations and evaluation of *future* conditions in the organization. This is one of several reasons why satisfaction is not a stronger predictor of turnover. For example, a management trainee may be very dissatisfied with his/her present job, but does not search for another job or quit because (s)he expects a more satisfying role in the organization in the future. Such future-oriented expectations and evaluations are covered by the second major determinant of turnover intentions and behavior — expected utility of alternative jobs within the organization.

Expected Utility of Internal Roles

Although an employee may currently be dissatisfied, turnover may not occur even though other jobs are available. The individual may expect that the present job will change or lead to more satisfying roles in the future. Such future-oriented expectations and evaluations can be based on: expected changes in the present job; expected transfer possibilities; expected promotions; expected changes in organizational policies, practices or conditions (such as changes in pay, job content, or management, etc.); and/or expected transfer, promotion, or turnover among other individuals.

The management trainee, the basic-training military recruit, the junior faculty member, the low-seniority employee, and the night-shift worker, are some of the individuals who may be dissatisfied with their present job but who do not quit because of positive expectations about future roles in the organization.

It is important to recognize that just as the dissatisfied employee may not quit, given positive expectations about future roles in the organization, the currently satisfied employee who has negative expectations about the future in the organization may quit. For example, expected negative changes in the job, the lack of perceived desirable promotional opportunities, and expected negative changes in policy, practices, or conditions may lead currently satisfied employees to seek external jobs.

While satisfaction is based on *multiple* individual values and *current* perceptions, expected utility of alternative internal roles is based on *multiple* individual values and *future* expectations of policies, practices, conditions and outcomes in the organization. Thus in diagnosing turnover, it is necessary to assess not only the employee's current satisfaction but also the employee's expectations about future roles in the organization based on the work values most important to the individual.

Expected Utility of External Alternative Work Roles

This variable, the third major determinant of turnover, seeks to capture the individual's expectation of finding an attractive alternative job external to the present organization. The dissatisfied employee and/or the employee with low expectations regarding internal alternatives may not quit because attractive external jobs are not perceived. Conversely, the satisfied employee and/or the employee with positive expectations regarding internal alternatives may quit because a highly attractive external job is perceived (for example via an executive search firm).

Expected utility of external jobs is based on: the employee's important work values; expected attainment of these values from the external job(s); and expectation of being able to attain the alternative job(s). Thus a more complete diagnosis and understanding of turnover requires assessment of this variable.

It is interesting to note that many organizations do detailed comparative analyses of pay and benefits in their industry and relevant labor markets. From the perspective of employee turnover, this model suggests it would be useful to expand this competitive analysis to other work rewards, outcomes, and conditions. At a minimum, employee perceptions of the rewards, outcomes, and conditions available from external alternatives would be useful diagnostic information.

Nonwork Values and Roles

The preceding three determinants of turnover — satisfaction expectation regarding jobs internal to the organization, and expected utility of external jobs — are based on the individual's *work values* in relation to present job and alternative internal or external roles. Missing from this framework are potentially important *nonwork values* and *roles.* Whether or not individuals translate their present and future evaluation of the job and alternatives into turnover intentions and behavior, may be related to the degree to which the job or alternatives are perceived or expected to facilitate or interfere with important nonwork values and/or conflict with nonwork roles. As with work values, individual differences must be recognized. For individuals whose central life values are nonwork-related, (Dubin *et al.,* 1975), their job choice and turnover decision would be expected to be less strongly related to the work value-based evaluations discussed under the three preceding determinants. Conversely, for individuals whose central life values are predominantly work-related, the relationships among the three preceding determinants and turnover should be stronger. For most individuals, there will probably be a mix of work and nonwork values involved in the turnover decision. Family orientation, life-style and geographical preferences, and religious, cultural, altruistic, athletic, and social values will be interrelated with work-related values.

Thus the understanding, prediction, and management of turnover requires the assessment of the importance of nonwork values and roles and the extent to which policies, practices, and conditions are perceived by employees (or prospective employees) to facilitate or interfere with the attainment of nonwork values.

Transfer policies, rotating shifts, travel requirements, fixed work hours, and leave-of-absence policies, are examples of policies, practices, and conditions which may influence potentially important nonwork values and roles. Further, the increased incidence of dual-career families (Bailyn, 1970; Rapoport and Rapoport, 1976) requires the assessment of the impact of policies, practices, and conditions not only on employees, but also employees' spouses.

As noted in the preceding chapter, there is relatively little empirical research on nonwork values and roles in the turnover process. The model discussed here suggests that this area requires detailed explanation if turnover is to be more fully understood and effectively managed.

Alternative Forms of Withdrawal

Turnover and other behaviors such as absenteeism and apathy are often grouped under the same generic label of "withdrawal" behavior. It is accurate that turnover represents physical withdrawal from the organization. However, it is not accurate to describe all turnover as withdrawal if what is being implied is escape-motivated behavior (Mobley, 1982). As noted above, turnover may occur among satisfied employees who are attracted by the highly positive expectations of an external job or who decide to pursue nonwork values.

However, when an individual wishes to quit an undesirable job (but is constrained, for example, by the lack of attractive alternative jobs, by external factors such as spouse's career, or by contractual constraints), alternative forms of withdrawal may be expected in the form of absenteeism, apathy, etc. Thus these alternative behaviors may be diagnostic with respect to turnover in that turnover may occur when and if the constraints are removed. (See Mobley, 1980 for an expanded discussion of the turnover-absenteeism relationship).

Other Variables

As illustrated in Fig. 6.5, employee perceptions of organizational policies, practices and conditions, perceptions of the labor market, and individual differences in values, expectations, and personal and occupational variables are the precursors of satisfaction, expected utility of present role, expected utility of alternatives, and relevance of nonwork values. In the previous chapter we reviewed the research related to a number of these variables.

Evaluation

The expanded Mobley *et al.* (1979) model has yet to be empirically evaluated. The number of the suggested relationships are conceptually appealing and have indirect empirical support. Given the complexity of the model, it is unlikely that any one study will adequately evaluate the model. The intent of this model was to graphically examine the turnover process. It remains for future conceptual and empirical work to assess the adequacy with which this complexity is represented. From the managerial perspective, this model calls attention to the fact that satisfaction, future expectations, and both work and nonwork values must be diagnosed if turnover is to be understood and managed.

SUMMARY

In this chapter we have presented four conceptual models of the employee turnover process. From a theoretical perspective, each model has contributed to the integration of the voluminous turnover literature, has focused on the multiple determinants of turnover, and has stimulated consideration of turnover as a process over time. As we will discuss in the last chapter, research and analysis designs which effectively capture this complex process continue to be needed.

It is important that managers and researchers recognize the complexity portrayed in these models. Since there are multiple determinants of turnover, multiple strategies for effectively diagnosing and managing turnover are required. Simplistic diagnoses and panacea prescriptions will not lead to effective management of turnover.

Toward a Further Understanding of Employee Turnover

7

INTRODUCTION

This final chapter is devoted to highlighting some major gaps in our understanding of employee turnover and looking briefly to the future. The preceding chapters have drawn on a broad body of literature dealing with theory, research, and practice. A great deal is known about employee turnover. The challenges before us are to develop this body of knowledge further, to address the voids in the body of knowledge, and to translate this body of knowledge into more effective management, of employee turnover in particular, and of human resources in general.

FURTHER RESEARCH NEEDS

A major void in our understanding of the turnover processes lies in the area of consequences. In Chapters 1 and 2 we illustrated a variety of possible positive and negative turnover consequences. However, other consequences and the interrelationships among consequences remain to be specified. We need to develop measurement technologies for integrating these consequences into composite utility indexes. If turnover is to be understood and effectively managed, the desirable or undesirable cost-benefit of multiple consequences needs immediate and ingenious attention.

With respect to the causes of turnover, a variety of factors have been identified. However, several weaknesses remain evident. First, turnover is too frequently analyzed in terms of only one or a small number of potential causes. Since most of the possible causes of turnover are not independent, such simple analyses do not permit identification of the relative importance of various factors. Continued emphasis on multivariate research is warranted. This need for multivariate analysis and reporting is applicable to theoretical turnover research, within-organization turnover research, and the comparative turnover data publicly reported by groups such as the Department of Labor and the Bureau of National Affairs.

A third void in our understanding of turnover is the role of performance. As noted in previous chapters, from a managerial perspective, it would seem obvious that the organizational consequences of turnover are intimately associated with the performance level of the leavers. However, in exploring the turnover analysis practices of private-sector organizations, we find that relatively few organizations incorporate performance into their internal analysis and reporting of turnover. As previously discussed, the literature exhibits a dearth of conceptual or empirical treatments of performance as either an antecedent or consequence in the turnover process.

A variety of subquestions follow from the general inquiry into the role of performance in the turnover processes. The examples include:

a. Do high performers have and perceive more external alternatives?

b. Do high performers with a desire or intent to leave modify their performance in the absence of perceived external alternative jobs?

c. Do nonperformance-contingent reward systems encourage turnover among high performers?

d. What are the consequences for stayers of the departure of individuals of differing performance levels?

e. How can the utility of turnover among individuals of differing performance levels be indexed?

Porter and Steers (1973) and Mobley (1980, 1982) argue that future turnover research should distinguish between effective and ineffective leavers. This argument, largely unheeded, continues to be relevant in our attempts to understand the turnover process more fully.

A fourth continuing concern is the relative lack of research emphasis on turnover as a process. While the conceptual models reviewed in Chapter 6 are process models, little of our research assesses this process directly. By dictionary definition, a process is: (a) a phenomenon marked by changes that lead to a particular result; (b) a series of actions or operations leading to an end. Inherent in this definition are change, time, actions, and operations. In the case of turnover, these actions and operations may be behavioral, cognitive or affective. The causes and consequences of turnover change and interact over time. Turnover is an ongoing process, rather than a static event.

Examine our typical turnover research design. We collect data on possible causes, usually from surveys and personnel records, at one point in time; later we collect the turnover criterion data, and then perform correlational analysis on the two sets of data.

At the time we collect our survey measures, individuals may be at different points in the turnover process. In the interval between our single survey measure and collection of the turnover data, the individuals' perceptions, preferences, and evaluations of self, organization, and alternatives may have changed. There may be individual differences in process time based on, for example, preference for immediate or delayed gratification. There may also be a number of feedback loops among turnover antecedents, such as satisfaction and success of search (see Mobley, 1977). The point is that our one-time measures and subsequent correlational analysis miss the bulk of the process in the turnover process.

If we are to understand the process of turnover more fully, we need repeated measures of multiple antecedents over time and statistical analyses which include the temporal dimension. Multiple surveys, employee diaries, repeated observations, researcher-employee interaction on a continuing or regular basis, and cohort analyses of stayers and leavers are possible alternatives to the convenient but inadequate single-administration measures. The work of Porter, Crampon and Smith (1977), Graen and Ginsburgh (1977), and Youngblood, Laughlin, Mobley, and Meglino (1980) (each using a different variate of a longitudinal design), illustrate the types of paradigms required if we are to make progress in understanding turnover as a process. Organizations would be well advised to follow cohorts from the time of organizational entry into their careers, in order to gain greater insight into the turnover (and career development) process.

A fifth continuing research need, related to the process argument, concerns the relationship between turnover and other withdrawal behaviors such as absenteeism or apathy. Can absenteeism be a safety valve, allowing work pressures to dissipate and thus reduce the desire or need to quit? While there is ample speculation on the possible relationships among turnover and other withdrawal behaviors, there is relatively little strong conceptual and empirical research. From both theoretical and programatic perspectives, these possible relationships deserve greater attention.

The sixth and final continuing research need to be discussed here concerns the relative lack of experimental or quasi-experimental research. Much of our turnover research is based on correlational analysis which precludes causal statements. Experimental and quasi-experimental research, while difficult, is needed. Hulin's (1968) study of the turnover effects of changes in job satisfaction; Krackhardt et al.'s (1981) study of supervisory interactions and turnover; and the realistic job preview experiments reviewed by Horner (1979) and Wanous (1980) demonstrate the feasibility and utility of experimental designs in turnover research.

THE MANAGER AS RESEARCHER

"What is an appropriate level of turnover for this company?" The preceding chapters should serve to underscore the fact that this frequently heard question has no simple answer. The labor market, the occupations in question, the consequences, the performance of stayers and leavers, the cost of turnover reduction strategies, etc., relate to the answer of this question. The fallacy of an organization-wide turnover goal should be evident. The previous chapters should also serve to underscore the naivety of assuming that any single policy, practice, or program will be adequate for effectively managing turnover.

One theme of this book has been that the effective management of turnover requires a diagnostic-evaluative perspective. The variety of possible turnover cases and consequences require systematic diagnosis, hypothesis formulation, development and implementation of turnover management strategies, and evaluation of the cost-benefits of such strategies.

In turnover management, as with many other areas of managerial concern, the role of researcher is imbedded in the managerial role. The preceding discussions of causes, concepts, consequences, and control have sought to provide the manager with a framework for researching and managing turnover.

A LOOK TO THE FUTURE

The interest in employee turnover, evident in past years, will probably expand in the future. Continued inflation and growth in human resource costs will require increasingly sophisticated human resource measurement systems, including turnover costs and consequences. The post-baby-boom labor market of the late 1980s and 1990s (Wachter, 1980; Wernick and McIntire, 1980) will be, in Drucker's (1980) terms, a source of turbulence. The decline in the relative number of young people entering the work force indicates a competitive and multialternative labor market.

Further, with the extension of mandatory retirement, longer life-expectancies, and the aging of the baby-boom cohort, promotional and career advancement opportunities may be constrained. The potential implications of these developments on turnover are apparent.

In conclusion, we have important questions yet to answer regarding turnover; the individual and organizational importance of the turnover process will become even more salient in the coming decades. Understanding the concepts and consequences of turnover is more important than ever. Hopefully, the diagnostic approach suggested in this book will assist the student and manager in the continuing pursuit of this understanding.

Appendix

FORCE-LOSS COST ANALYSIS*
H.W. Gustafson†

"Ah, make the most of what we yet may spend . . ."
— *Rubaiyat*

INTRODUCTION

Basis of the Problem

Some decades ago the Studebaker automobile company was given to publishing advertisements picturing, as I recall, three generations of one family all employed simultaneously at the same factory, with a small boy thrown in the bargain to presage a like destiny for generation number four. Evidently someone in Studebaker's advertising department felt this would appeal to the American sense of the essential fitness of things, and possi-

*Copyright © 1980 by the American Telephone and Telegraph Company. The views expressed here are the author's and not necessarily those of his employer, the American Telephone and Telegraph Company.

†The work reported is a product of the labors of over 20 Bell System employees and more than a half-dozen consultants, all of whom have contributed important substantive ideas as well as perspiration. Regrettably, it is not possible to acknowledge the individual contributions of so many people. I hope all will realize, however, that their efforts have not gone unappreciated.

bly it did. At the time, the attitude reflected by the ads was consonant with conditions. Business and industry were experiencing unprecedented work-force stability destined to endure some 35 years (circa 1925–1960), interrupted only, and briefly, by the second World War. In many companies throughout this period, rates of work-force turnover were sufficiently low to lend more than a little credence to the advertising theme.

No such image of the work force would arouse much sympathy nowadays, however. Indeed, the image seemed incongruous with the American spirit, if not economic reality, even then. For the goal of occupational mobility has played a prominent role in the ethos of the nation as far back at least as the early half of the 19th century. If stability of employment has often been the fact, mobility as often has been the dream. Where, in the past, strivings for occupational movement were tied most closely to desires for socioeconomic betterment, more recently they have become linked equally to aspirations for personal satisfaction and fulfillment. Jointly these objectives have succeeded in driving the Studebaker point of view off the market. If employment in a single job from cradle to the grave did once exist as a cultural ideal, it has vanished from the scene long since, as extinct as the Studebaker car.

In the Bell Telephone System, as elsewhere, it is still the case that many employees retire annually, having served in the same occupation for 30 to 40 years. To the extent that employment is a matter of choice, such longevity is a consequence of preference; and no doubt there always will be large numbers of people who elect to devote their working careers to a single job. All the same, occupational stability, as a societal aim, has effectively disappeared. To change jobs, even frequently, is no longer improper or unethical; little if any stigma attaches itself to the mobile worker.

Since the 1950s, work force turnover has risen sharply above the levels of previous years. It is hard to be certain, but there is reason to believe this increase in turnover is, in the main, an outgrowth of modern standards regarding occupational mobility, rather than merely a temporary aberration of an inflationary economy. If so, business and industry must look to a future of continuing high turnover which, as the experience of the

1960s has shown, can generate serious problems if not understood as thoroughly, and managed as effectively, as possible.

Over and above confronting continued high rates of workforce turnover, many businesses, the Bell System included, have taken steps to institutionalize higher rates of job mobility inside the corporate body by inaugurating upgrade and transfer programs to facilitate job changes. Mechanisms for internal mobility always have existed, of course, but the machinery now is more formal, systematic, and public than ever before. The long-term effects of these programs obviously cannot be known for years to come, but their impact on both internal and external turnover may prove substantial. It is a truism that nearly every transfer or promotion creates behind it a chain reaction of job openings requiring several further personnel replacements to be made.

In brief, high rates of employee turnover promise to remain a permanent fact of business life. Improved techniques of dealing with these higher rates of turnover are therefore in order. This paper deals with one such technique called "Force-Loss Cost Analysis," or FLCA.

Costs of Turnover

Commentators on work-force turnover not uncommonly tend to regard it as a problem in need of remedy, especially turnover deriving from resignations and dismissals. This attitude may be correct, although the basis for such a position is not always clear. Usually the reason given is that employee replacement costs are high. No one knows very accurately what these replacement costs amount to, but it is certain that in the United States they run to many billions of dollars per year. The Bell System alone replaces well in excess of 100,000 employees yearly, and data to be presented later will show that the outlay for this is unquestionably greater than $1000 per occurrence.

But the fact that the cost is high does not mean automatically that replacement of personnel is bad economics. Given the capital to make such action feasible, no rational businessperson would hesitate to replace $100,000,000 worth of equipment every year if he was confident that the new equipment would

reduce maintenance expenses and increase productivity sufficiently to return a good profit on the investment. He would make
the replacement in that case because he understands — or, at any
rate, feels he understands — the probable economic consequences of his action.

In the case of work-force turnover, however, it is not possible
for a businessperson to think or behave as he would with respect
to investment of capital, because neither the cost of turnover nor
its economic ramifications are well understood. It is a rare manager indeed who has more than the vaguest idea how much it
costs to replace an employee, what effect the replacement will
have on productivity, or how much longevity to anticipate on the
part of the new replacement. In light of the large sums known to
be involved, it behooves the business community, in my opinion,
to try to learn more about these matters and to put the answers to
use as fast as possible. Which is where the technique of force-loss
cost analysis (FLCA) enters in. The purpose of this paper is to
demonstrate how force-loss cost analysis, judiciously applied,
can lead to significantly improved understanding of work-force
turnover, both its costs and economic effects. For a more concise,
theoretical treatment of much the same ideas, see Bassett.[1]

Current Status

Although the ensuing discussion of FLCA is illustrated liberally
with data drawn from actual applications, it should be made plain
that the project is still in a research and development mode. FLCA
has not been implemented operationally on a day-to-day basis in
the Bell System. Whether, or how soon, implementation will take
place is a matter for conjecture.

There is an awkward stage akin to adolescence that inter-
venes between development of any new technology and its application in the field. During this stage, communication failures
breed confusion, resistance to change constrains progress, over-
zealous selling causes suspicion, and misuses are interpreted as
faults in the technology. This is the current status of FLCA. Hopefully, the present paper will assist in giving FLCA direction and
moving it on its way to useful application.

Rules of Costing

Prior to commencement of research on FLCA in 1971, numerous isolated studies of turnover costs had been conducted at various times throughout the Bell System, each yielding a different answer. Consequently, it became an early research objective to resolve previous discrepancies by identifying the "true" cost of turnover. After struggling for several weeks to formalize this objective in operational terms, meanwhile acquiring a nodding acquaintance with the rudiments of cost accounting, we realized that the quest was quixotic. For, as accountants know but psychologists may not, there is no such animal as the true cost of anything. Costs are calculated according to rules; the rules are set by people; and people may differ in the rules they set. We subsequently also learned, as accountants already know, that seemingly small alterations in the rules sometimes can generate large differences in the answers obtained.

Thus having rediscovered that cost accounting is not an exact science, we reformulated the initial objective as follows:

1. Model the rules used in FLCA after the cost accounting practices the Bell System currently applies to capital plant and equipment. Where no precedent exists, invoke rules that represent good practice in the eyes of professional accountants.

2. In computing costs, employ only objective data such as can withstand scrutiny by conscientious auditors.

3. Build an audit trial, including documentation of all arithmetic formulas and procedures.

4. Regard the resulting cost figures as the best available operational definition of "true" cost.

Because the rules of costing adopted in FLCA may diverge from the rules others would deem proper, not a little space is devoted in what follows to details of procedure. This seems necessary in order to convey a reasonably full flavor of FLCA not just to a general audience but to readers who may have special knowledge of cost accounting. Wherever possible, however, details are suppressed in favor of a more conceptual presentation.

OVERVIEW OF FLCA

The fundamental axiom of FLCA, borrowed from human resource accounting, is that the costs incurred in hiring and training employees should be capitalized rather than written off as current expense. In FLCA, the capital accounts are segregated by job classification, and in most applications are segregated also by organizational entity. Although accounting on an individual employee basis may be desirable for some purposes, one or two of which will be discussed later, group average accounting procedures are used primarily. Group average accounting corresponds in the main to the "positional" accounting discussed by other authors.[2]

On the occurrence of turnover due to resignation, dismissal, disability retirement, or death, the unamortized remainder of the associated investment is treated as operating loss. When turnover within a job classification arises from lateral transfer, promotion, or demotion, the investment remaining is transferred to the account identified with the new job and organizational entity.

Replacement Cost

The jobs chiefly of interest from the standpoint of FLCA are, of course, those with large populations and high turnover. In the Bell System most such occupations are production jobs involving repetitive performance of the same or similar tasks. Some examples are:

1. The Operator, who handles telephone calls placed by customers.

2. The Frameworker, who connects customer telephone lines to the switching network.

3. The Service Representative, who takes orders from customers for new, or modified, telephone service.

4. The Service Order Clerk, who processes customer orders to ensure proper billing.

In such occupations, the employee usually achieves mastery of the job in a relatively short time — as a rule of thumb, say two years or less. After mastery is attained, efficiency and quality of performance become the main criteria of productivity, rather than acquisition of new skills or knowledge. New learning, to be sure, is required in every job — e.g., when changes occur in operating practices — but in production jobs it is generally true that the cost of instilling this new learning is negligible alongside the initial costs of hiring and training.

For this reason, FLCA uses a procedure for computing employee investment that we have termed the "fixed tenure method," wherein investment is considered to cease accruing after the new employee has achieved a fixed tenure in the job. All employee costs beyond that time limit are regarded as operating expense. The alternative, obviously, would be a "variable tenure method," in which certain costs continue to be treated as investment over a variable, perhaps indefinite, period.

By definition, investment stops accruing under the fixed tenure method at the time the average new employee reaches job mastery. It turns out that establishing this cutoff point is one of the most difficult problems in FLCA. More will be said about this issue below.

Current replacement cost, or just *replacement cost,* is defined as the average total outlay required at present to hire and develop new employees to the point of job mastery. Since it takes time for a new worker to achieve job mastery, replacement cost is not an instantaneous expenditure, but builds up over an interval of weeks or months (even years, for some jobs). Whereas employment costs have already been incurred, or sunk, at the time the employee goes on the payroll, the costs of training and development have not. If it requires, say, six months for the average employee to reach job mastery, then anyone who leaves the job in less than six months has not yet built up an investment account equal to the full replacement cost. The portion of replacement cost accrued to the time of departure from the job is called *investment accumulated, disregarding amortization,* or simply *investment accumulated.* The fictitious data of Table 1 illustrate how the investment accumulated might aggregate month by month for a given job until it reaches the full replacement cost. In this example, the replacement cost is assumed to be $2795.

The expression "investment accumulated, disregarding amortization" should be understood to mean investment accumulated up to any specified time, assuming that no amortization of the account has taken place. Inasmuch as this assumption is, generally speaking, contrary to fact (all FLCA investment accounts are subject to amortization), investment accumulated is a convenient fiction used for explanatory purposes, not an actual monetary account.

Since turnover often occurs before full replacement cost has accrued — or before a full year of employment has elapsed, whichever is shorter — very inexact cost figures would result from use of the conventional annual accounting period for amortization. A one-month accounting period has therefore been chosen for FLCA. This not only makes the computations more precise, but facilitates frequent reporting of results.

Some arithmetical exercises have been done to find out if it makes any difference whether replacement cost is treated as a lump sum investment or broken into increments *a la* investment

TABLE 1

Illustration of investment accumulation, disregarding amortization

Months in Job	New Investment	Investment Accumulated	Proportion of Replacement Cost
1	$977	$ 977	35.0%
2	600	1577	56.4
3	576	2153	77.0
4	378	2531	90.6
5	210	2741	98.1
6	54	2795	100.0

accumulated. We have found that the answer depends on the choice of amortization algorithm, but the cost results obtained are somewhat divergent, at least, under any amortization procedure. We have consequently opted for the added precision afforded by handling investment cumulatively.

Except possibly for the on-job costs discussed later, the components comprising FLCA replacement cost are fairly standard. Since definitions are readily available elsewhere[1,2,3,4], there seems little reason to re-enumerate them here.

Investment Recovered and Lost

The investment accumulated in an individual consists at any instant of two parts, the proportion previously amortized and the unamortized remainder. The former is called *investment recovered*. When turnover occurs, the unamortized remainder is considered *investment lost* or *investment transferred,* depending on whether the turnover is external to the company or internal.

The basic accounting equation of FLCA, therefore, is:

Investment Accumulated = Investment Recovered
+ Investment Lost (or Transferred).

Since amortization is calculated monthly, the Investment Recovered term in this equation ordinarily is zero only during the first month. Thereafter it becomes nonzero and increases monotonically. The behavior of the Investment Lost term is, however, less predictable inasmuch as Accumulated Investment itself is monotone increasing up to the point of job mastery, i.e., when accumulated investment becomes equal to replacement cost. For every job studied to date, Investment Lost increases for a number of months before it starts its inevitable steady decline, and it is not unreasonable to expect that the same pattern might hold for all jobs.

Though theoretically important, the basic equation is not very helpful in practice. Simple as it may look, its behavior can be extremely complicated depending on the amortization algorithm and the rate of buildup of Investment Accumulated. As a result, it has not seemed worthwhile to try to fathom its mysteries by mathematical analysis. It is easier to compute and tabulate the answers step by step.

Traditionally, it has been customary to use the constant figure, replacement cost, as the measure of turnover cost. In FLCA, as can be seen from the basic equation, replacement cost is not a representative indicator of the cost of turnover. Many people leave their jobs before full replacement cost has accrued; and except when turnover takes place in the first few days, some prior amortization of investment always occurs. Accordingly, FLCA treats turnover cost as a variable whose value depends on the particular case.

Cost versus Value

One of the more difficult conceptual problems in FLCA has been, and continues to be, to understand the difference between the sunk costs of employee replacement, on the one side, and the asset values of human resource accounting, on the other. This distinction arises because ordinarily an employee, unlike capital equipment, is expected to increase in asset value, or worth to the business, with increased job experience and maturity. Though this view may derive in part from nostalgic attachment to the outmoded Studebaker ethic, it is widely espoused and there is much to be said for it. Under FLCA, however, apart from the characteristic early growth in investment discussed above, the unamortized investment in any employee diminishes steadily with time. In other words, as the employee's asset value grows, his FLCA investment account declines.

Officially, we shrug off this seeming paradox by observing that the sunk costs with which FLCA deals have little to do with employee value or worth. When turnover occurs, the investment lost — we say — does not represent the current worth of the asset lost, only the (depreciated) current cost of the company's investment in the asset. This, I believe, is a satisfactory argument from the standpoints both of cost accounting and forensics. But from the points of view of turnover analysis and abstract philosophy, such an answer begs the question. It would be far more desirable to possess a suitable accounting procedure for bridging the gap between worth and investment.

Several methods have been proposed for evaluating the enhancement in an employee's worth due to experience and maturity. I lack the accounting expertise to do these proposals justice and will not attempt to survey them, but would like to outline one very simple, perhaps naive, method suggested within the Bell System* that I have not seen described before in the literature.

The economic philosophy underlying this method is that in the long run, employees in a free, competitive marketplace are paid what they are worth. This is why their wages generally increase as they gain experience in a job. Their wage increases therefore may be regarded both as a measure of their augmented value to the business and as an investment on the part of their employer in securing this added worth. Hence, were the cumulative current cost of each employee's wage increases to be treated as investment and added to his FLCA account, the depreciated total would be a fair reflection of his present worth.

To illustrate concretely, suppose an employee receives wage increases of $250 each year for four years. The cumulative cost of these increases would be as shown in Table 2.

The table indicates that in addition to present FLCA investment accrual, some $250 of wage-increase investment would be accrued in the second year of employment, $500 in the third year, $750 in the fourth year, and $1000 in every subsequent year. The effect would be to add investment throughout the entire job tenure of the employee (variable tenure method), rather than to terminate accruals at the point of job mastery.

Admittedly, this approach to asset valuation has loopholes, not the least of which is the presumed long-run equitability of the competitive labor market. Nevertheless, the proposal is not entirely without promise, and would be extraordinarily simple to apply in practice.

---

*Due, evidently, to J. Holobovich and E. Viscardi of AT&T. The exact origins appear to be lost in antiquity.

TABLE 2
Illustration of additions to employee cost due to wage increases

YEAR ON THE JOB

		1	2	3	4	Each year thereafter
Wage increase		Added cost				
First	0	$250	$250	$250	$ 250
Second	0	0	250	250	250
Third	0	0	0	250	250
Fourth	0	0	0	0	250
Cumulative added cost	0	$250	$500	$750	$1,000

Efficiency Recovery Cost

The cutoff point for accumulation of investment under FLCA's fixed-tenure accrual method is established empirically for any job by determining the "proficiency acquisition curve" as exemplified in Fig. 1. Initially, a new employee exhibits a low level of productivity, then improves with practice until achieving job mastery. The shaded area above the proficiency acquisition curve represents production lost on the part of a new worker owing to inexperience. The cost of this lost production is called *efficiency recovery cost.* When turnover occurs among experienced employees, efficiency recovery cost is part of the price the employer has to pay to restore the work group to the level of productivity it previously enjoyed. The term "efficiency recovery" thus is applicable from the viewpoint of the employer, the term "proficiency acquisition" from that of the worker.

Efficiency recovery cost is not to be confused with experience cost as discussed above. Efficiency recovery cost arises out

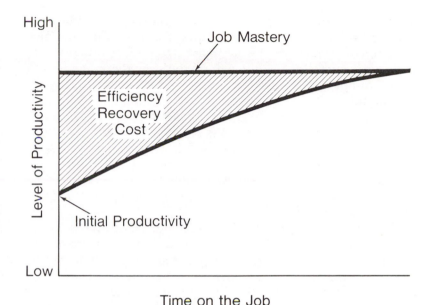

Fig. 1. *Hypothetical proficiency acquisition curve, illustrating the definition of efficiency recovery cost.*

of measurable improvements in productivity as an employee's skill develops; experience cost — which, as noted, is not now included in FLCA but might conceivably be measured by wage increases — derives from subtler, less tangible improvements in job performance that emanate from sheer survival on the job. The latter might encompass such intangibles, e.g., as increased loyalty to the company or enhanced ability to cope with rare types of emergency.

APPLICATIONS OF FLCA

In seeking support at AT&T for the FLCA research project, the position was taken originally that the main application would be to measure the performance of managers in controlling work-force turnover. Supervisors would be made accountable for turnover costs through appropriate allocation and monitoring of expense budgets and capital accounts. This would put the phenomenon of turnover on the same fiscal footing as other phases of business operations, at the same time simplifying the reporting of turnover statistics and making those statistics more meaningful.

I continue to believe that FLCA possesses potential as a tool for measuring how effectively supervisors manage the human resources at their disposal. At present, however, this application has been moved well down from topmost position in the schedule of priorities. It would be a cumbersome undertaking at best, and the likelihood of a favorable immediate payoff appears questionable.

The reason is compound. For one thing, all too little is known about the causes of work-force turnover, particularly voluntary resignations, even among lifelong researchers, let alone the operating managers of a business enterprise. Hence, it is difficult to supply supervisors with valid guidance on how to manage turnover. In addition, measurement of any kind, however well accepted by some managers, is always a threat to others. One need only visualize hordes of threatened supervisors initiating personnel-affecting activities on the strength of invalid advice, to appreciate the danger that FLCA as a stand-alone measurement device might prove counterproductive.

What is needed to control work-force turnover is, of course, a better understanding of what brings it about, accompanied by an overall system of manpower planning and supervisory training consistent with this understanding. FLCA then can find its proper niche in such a system as a way of measuring not just the effectiveness of supervisors, but the effectiveness of the system as a whole.

The Bell System has under way many operational programs and research projects oriented toward the objective of improved turnover management. Some of these programs and projects aim at reducing turnover (e.g., job enrichment, job/person matching), others at increasing it (e.g., skill upgrading, assessment of potential). It is in the evaluation and optimization of efforts such as these that FLCA's promise now, on more mature reflection, seems to me to lie; the next few sections review several of these potential applications in detail.

Initial versus On-Job Training

Relatively few employees at time of hire possess the technical skills to perform telephone company jobs. They are selected on the basis of general suitability for a given type of work, then trained in the specific skills their jobs require. In most cases, this training is conducted off the job by an instructor other than the supervisor to whom the employee ultimately will report. It is called "initial training," in contradistinction to training administered later, on the job, under the aegis of the line supervisor. Depending on the job, initial training may consume anywhere from a few hours to several months of time.

It is fairly easy to determine the cost of initial training. The cost of on-job training, however, is harder to ascertain. Much of it is informal and is administered intermittently as the need arises. For this reason we have elected in FLCA to define the cost of on-job training operationally as consisting of two components. The first is efficiency recovery cost, encountered earlier; the second is extra supervision cost. Just as efficiency recovery cost is the fraction of worker wages paid for production not achieved prior to job mastery (cf. Fig. 1), so extra supervision cost is the fraction of supervisor wages paid for extra time devoted to new employees during the same period. In both cases the wages are loaded to cover the costs of any materials and facilities utilized.

Since efficiency recovery need not be due exclusively to training, it is more precise to define the sum of efficiency recovery cost and extra supervision cost as the cost of on-job *learning* rather than on-job *training*.

Training trade-offs.   Most people would accept it as axiomatic that initial training has an effect on on-job learning and that, between the components of on-job learning, extra supervision has an impact on efficiency recovery. I am unaware of any data to support this proposition, but it is logical and very possibly true. Certainly, at any rate, it is in the best interests of trainers and supervisors to believe that it is true. So stipulating, then, there ought to be some optimum distribution of cost among these factors, and managers ought to be interested in knowing what the optimum balance is. Perhaps, for instance, a heavier emphasis on initial training would effectuate sufficient reduction in efficiency recovery cost and/or extra supervision cost to more than offset the added cost of the augmented initial training. Or conversely, maybe a substantial reduction could be made in initial training without occasioning a proportionate increase in the costs of on-job learning.

In conducting such a trade-off analysis, it is not enough to look at replacement costs; it is necessary to consider the turnover pattern as well. For when turnover occurs early, say just after initial training, the entire investment accumulated becomes an operating loss; but because no on-job learning costs have accrued, the amount lost is comparatively small. In contrast, when turnover takes place later, the operating loss may be larger, but the loss is offset to some degree through prior amortization.

This is illustrated in Table 3, which shows the amount of investment in initial training and on-job learning recovered and lost in the event of turnover by a prototypical telephone operator after two months, and again after 18 months, on the job. Although the total amount lost on these three components of investment is about the same in both cases ($1162 as against $1071), one-third (32.7 percent) of the investment accumulated has been recovered at 18 months, but only 4.3 percent at two months. In this example, ten two-month employees would have to turn over, at an operating loss of $11,620 (10 × $1162), to recover the same amount of investment recovered on one 18-month operator. Thus, the optimum replacement cost is not necessarily the minimum replacement cost. If a great deal of turnover takes place shortly after hire, it is conceivable that the best cost balance might be struck by minimizing initial training even at the expense of sizable increases in on-job learning costs.

To make the issue still more complex, it is not improbable that initial training and extra supervision themselves have an

TABLE 3

Illustration of FLCA investment recovered and lost* after two and eighteen months of job tenure

AFTER 2 MONTHS

	Accumulated	Recovered	Lost
Initial training	$ 565	$29	$ 536
Efficiency recovery	451	17	444
Extra supervision	188	6	182
Total	$1214	$52	$1162

Percent investment recovered = 4.3%

AFTER 18 MONTHS

	Accumulated	Recovered	Lost
Initial training	$ 565	$196	$ 369
Efficiency recovery	715	226	489
Extra supervision	311	98	213
Total	$1591	$520	$1071

Percent investment recovered = 32.7%

*Transferred, rather than lost, in the event of internal turnover.

influence on patterns of turnover. If so, a change in the mix of training in order to optimize replacement costs with respect to the current pattern of turnover might alter that pattern to render the mix no longer optimal. The problem, therefore, is similar to that of optimizing the factors of production in a manufacturing operation; this, too, is very complicated, but that does not dissuade anybody from attempting to resolve it. The key to solving any problem is to have a rational, systematic means of attacking it. In respect to optimization of training costs, FLCA provides such a key.

An interesting example of training-cost optimization is cited by Gaudet[3] (pp. 49–50), in which large savings were realized by shifting emphasis from on-job learning to initial training. The analysis presented is deceptively simple, however, in that turnover was apparently unaffected and so could be ignored.

Other points.   Some miscellaneous points related to Table 3 should be noted in passing. First, the data in the table pertain to the job of Toll Operator, which is mastered by the average employee in less than 18 months. Hence, the investment accumulated column for the 18-month operators contains the replacement costs for the components listed. The total of $1591 is not, however, the full replacement cost, as the costs of recruiting, hiring, and separation have been omitted. Full replacement cost would come closer to $2000.

The figures shown are actual, but are based on a single locality in the Bell System and must not be construed as System averages. In other work locations the costs for the same job have been found to differ markedly from these. Nevertheless, the numbers in the table do fall in the general ballpark for Toll Operator, a job for which the replacement cost is quite low in comparison to many other telephone occupations. This supports the claim made earlier that the annual cost of replacing over 100,000 Bell System employees is in excess of $1000 each.

Many previous studies of turnover cost have dealt only with employment and initial training, omitting the costs of on-job learning. Based on the data in Table 3 as well as several similar studies, it begins to appear that the on-job costs, especially efficiency recovery, are always large in relation to other cost components. If so, any study that neglects them is suspect.

Finally, it should go without saying that trade-off analyses of initial training versus on-job learning have to take more factors than dollars alone into account. As one bad apple can spoil the barrel, so one poorly trained worker can spoil the output of a whole work group. Thus in conducting a trade-off analysis, care must be taken to ensure that the optimum cost balance from the standpoint of FLCA is not achieved at the expense of degradation in product quality.

The "Proficiency Gap"

No one can doubt that people differ in job performance. It follows, then, that individuals are consistent in job performance. For if inconsistent, there can be no typical performance levels by which employees can be compared. Strangely, however, there has been very little research on the consistency and variability of individual performance on the job. The studies available can be counted on the fingers of, at most, two hands.

One such investigation having to do with the productivity of telephone operators was conducted by AT&T not long ago.[5] Significant positive relationships were found between productivity during the first two weeks on the job and productivity at various subsequent times ranging up to six months later. For one work group the rank-order correlation at the six month point was as large as 0.83. Moreover, the absolute difference in productivity between top and bottom performers was as big after six months as it was initially. Hence, if the study can be generalized, it would seem that employees who are relatively high producers when first assigned to a job are likely to remain high producers later on.*

The difference in output between the relatively high and relatively low producers at any stage of job tenure has been termed "the proficiency gap" by one of my colleagues. The term is a misnomer to the degree that proficiency and actual perfor-

---

*H.F. Rothe, who has done more work on the consistency of job performance than anybody else, repeatedly has obtained for other occupations findings similar to those reported here, but interprets the results to be evidence of *inconsistency!* Apparently consistency is in the eye of the beholder. Cf., e.g., Rothe, "Output Rates among Coil Winders." In W.W. Ronan and E.P. Prien (eds.), *Perspectives on the Measurement of Human Performance.* (New York: Appleton-Century-Crofts, 1971). Reprinted from the *Journal of Applied Psychology,* 1958, **42,** 182−86.

mance diverge, but the proficiency/performance distinction need not concern us here. It can be very useful to know the size of the proficiency gap and whether it narrows or widens with job experience, for the answer can add another whole dimension to trade-off analyses of training costs.

For example, the above findings prompted a special calculation of efficiency recovery cost in which the operators were divided into two groups based on their median level of initial productivity. For both groups, job mastery was defined as the average level of productivity currently displayed by the experienced operators at the same work location.

Proficiency acquisition curves were plotted and efficiency recovery costs computed for both groups. For the high producers, efficiency recovery cost proved to be $499, and for the low producers, $1077. The proficiency gap, in other words, carried with it a cost of $1077 − $499 = $578, not counting any added extra supervision the low producers may have consumed. Since, as the study demonstrated, it appears possible to predict from the start who the low and high producers are going to be, it becomes a challenge to trainers and supervisors to make selective adjustments in initial training and extra supervision so as to optimize replacement costs not just in the aggregate, but for individual employees.

Costs associated with the proficiency gap can be calculated, of course, without reference to FLCA. Force-loss cost analysis comes into the picture because it is widely believed that workforce turnover and the proficiency gap are related. There are two theories. One is that the high producers turn over rapidly; the other is that the low producers do. I have no idea which theory, if either, is correct. The matter has not been investigated systematically. Probably it depends on the nature of the job itself along with a host of other variables. What is clear, however, is that FLCA provides a practical lever for exerting pressure on a refractory problem attended in the past by much lip service but little else. If trainers and supervisors can know ahead of time not only that one new job incumbent is going to cost more to develop than another, but that their probabilities of turnover are different, differential cost expectancies can be computed and the available decision alternatives exercised more rationally than heretofore.

Turnover Characteristics

Perhaps no type of statistic is bandied about more cavalierly than turnover rates. Hardly anyone hesitates to quote turnover percentages, or to compare the percentages one with another, at the drop of a hat. Almost invariably on close examination it turns out, however, that the figures cited have little bearing on the point at issue, or that the percentages compared are noncomparable. As demographers and labor economists are keenly aware, the characterization of turnover by statistical means is, in fact, an exceedingly complex problem[3,6]. No fully acceptable solution has been discovered, or is likely to be.

For purposes of FLCA we have adopted an approach called "annual rate by tenure category" which has a number of advantages, not the least being that it has been used in the Bell System for years and is familiar to many managers. The method is easiest explained by example.

Method of computation.   Suppose we are interested in the turnover rate among employees having more than three months, but not more than six months, of job tenure. These employees comprise the "three-to-six month tenure category." Suppose further that we want to describe their rate of turnover during a specified three-month base period, months A, B, and C. The following data are necessary:

1. The average number of members of the work force comprising the three-to-six month tenure category during the three-month base period. In practice we calculate this average by counting the number of three-to-six month employees at the start of each of months A, B, and C, then adding the counts together and dividing by three. The result is called the "average monthly force size" within the given tenure category. If greater precision is wanted, an average weekly force size or even an average daily force size may be computed.

2. The total number of force losses (i.e., the turnover) within the three-to-six month tenure category during the same base period.

Illustrative data, together with the ensuing percentage computation, might appear as follows:

Month	Number of Three-to-Six-Month Employees at Start of Month	Force Losses During Month
A	131	4
B	122	9
C	128	2
Total	381	15

Average monthly force size = 381/3 = 127.

Turnover rate during base period = 15/127 × 100 = 11.8%.

The resulting turnover rate of 11.8 percent is awkward to interpret because it represents an unconventional period of time, in this case three months. The final step, therefore, is to "annualize" the rate by extrapolating the base period to a full year. This is accomplished by assuming that if the base period had been four times longer, i.e., twelve months rather than three, the force losses would have increased four-fold to 4 × 15 = 60, but the average monthly force size would have remained the same. The annual rate of turnover for the three-to-six month tenure category then becomes 60/127 × 100 = 47.2 percent or, alternatively, 4 × 11.8% = 47.2 percent.

Turnover and tenure.   Computation of separate rates for different tenure categories is imperative because of the powerful relationship that obtains between turnover and tenure. Observe, for example, the data of Table 4(a) regarding the telephone operators in one city during the first nine months of 1971.

Clearly, for this city, and for this job, the overall annual turnover rate of 30.1 percent gives a poor characterization of the phenomenon. Turnover among brand new employees is four times the overall average, and among experienced operators,

TABLE 4(a)

Illustrative turnover data for telephone operators, one city, first nine months of 1971

TENURE CATEGORY

	Under 3 Months	3–6 Months	6–12 Months	Over 12 Months	All Tenures
Monthly average force size	14.7	16.7	50.3	255.2	336.9
Force losses*	15	14	19	28	76
Annual rate of turnover	136.0%	111.7%	50.4%	14.6%	30.1%

*Resignations and dismissals only.

only half the average. In none of the tenure categories shown does the rate approximate 30.1 percent.

It is true that this approach eventuates in a proliferation of numbers, the more so if figures are maintained separately for different types of turnover such as resignations, dismissals, and promotions. But it is difficult to think of a viable option. As in all statistical analyses, it is important to measure the dispersion as well as the central tendency.

Although this method of characterizing turnover is, in my opinion, very satisfactory, it still can be improved by superimposing FLCA information on the turnover rates as, for instance, in Table 4(b).

Many new interpretations of the data now can be made, depending on the purpose at hand. It can be seen, for instance, that the larger part of investment lost derives from resignations and dismissals not among new employees, but among moderately to highly experienced operators. This conclusion is tempered, of course, by the fact, from Table 4(a), that the bulk of the operators are found in the longer-tenure categories, and by the higher percentage of investment recovered through prior

TABLE 4(b)
Illustrative FLCA data for telephone operators, one city, first nine
months of 1971

TENURE CATEGORY

	Under 3 Months	3–6 Months	6–12 Months	Over 12 Months
Annual rate of turnover*	136.0%	111.7%	50.4%	14.6%
Annual total investment loss	$35,121	$27,888	$34,661	$37,187
% investment recovered	3.3%	10.2%	23.7%	41.8%

*Resignations and dismissals only.

amortization when turnover occurs in these categories. When
new employees turn over, on the other hand, any investment that
has been made in them is almost entirely wasted.

In the interest of minimizing this waste, efforts to reduce
turnover should be directed toward new operators, and it
scarcely requires either sophisticated turnover statistics or FLCA
information to tell anyone this. The main ingredient added by the
more detailed characterization of turnover is an indication of the
costs and benefits likely to be realized from efforts to alleviate
work-force loss. It is evident from Table 4(b), for example, that a
program designed to halve resignations and dismissals among
people having under three months' tenure cannot expect to be
profitable if the cost of operating the program exceeds
$35,121/2 = $17,560 per year. Which brings us to another, and
most important, prospective application of FLCA, cost-benefit
analysis.

Cost-Benefit Analysis

Cost-benefit analysis of programs designed to influence work-
force turnover ranks high in immediacy among the uses foreseen
for FLCA. Such programs may seek either to reduce resignations

and dismissals or to encourage transfers and promotions. Since evaluation of the latter type of program is somewhat more involved, the simpler case, turnover reduction, will be discussed first.

Experimental and control groups.   Imagine that a program to minimize resignations and dismissals has been instituted among a specified group of employees, to be known as the "experimental group." The scientific approach to cost-benefit analysis is then to identify another group of employees, the "control group," who resemble the experimental group in as many relevant particulars as possible, but are not exposed to the program. The criteria on which the matching of control group to experimental group are based are of course crucial, but for the sake of illustration, we may assume the matching has been properly done.

Two questions are of interest: (1) does the experimental group following advent of the program display a better turnover rate than the control group? and (2) If so, how much money is saved in consequence of the lowered turnover?

To fix ideas, consider the data in Tables 5(a), 5(b), and 5(c) relating to a company-sponsored child care center. The hypothesis is that the center will relieve working parents of child-care burdens, thereby prolonging their stay in the work force. Typically, such a center would be used by employee-parents from a variety of vocational groups, thus necessitating a separate cost-benefit analysis for each job represented. For simplicity of illustration, Tables 5(a), 5(b), and 5(c) deal only with a single telephone job, that of Service Representative.

The tables are based on a real program and reflect real cost figures for Service Representatives in one city. However, to enhance the example's instructive value, the turnover data have been manipulated by the writer. Consequently, no substantive interpretation is intended, or can be made, from the numbers shown.

Table 5(a) gives resignation and dismissal rates by tenure category for the experimental and control groups. It is meant to be understood that the table covers a full chronological year, so

TABLE 5(a)

1972 turnover among service representatives using and not using a company-sponsored child care center (fictitious data)

TENURE CATEGORY (MONTHS)	AVERAGE MONTHLY FORCE SIZE	RESIGNATIONS AND DISMISSALS	TURNOVER RATE (%)
Users of child care center—experimental group			
0–6	1.4	1	71.4%
6–12	2.2	1	45.5
12–18	3.6	1	27.8
18–30	6.1	0	0.0
30–42	6.1	1	16.4
42–60	6.4	1	15.6
60–96	3.6	0	0.0
Total	29.4	5	17.0%
Nonusers of child care center—control group			
0–6	2.1	1	47.6
6–12	4.3	1	23.3
12–18	2.8	1	35.7
18–30	7.6	1	13.2
30–42	8.1	1	12.3
42–60	7.2	2	27.8
60–96	5.7	1	17.5
Total	37.8	8	21.2%

no annualization of rates is necessary. The totals indicate that the aggregate (annual) resignation and dismissal rate for the experimental group, 17 percent, is somewhat better than the associated rate for the control group, 21.2 percent. On this information alone, ignoring questions of statistical reliability, one would

TABLE 5(b)
Predicted experimental group resignations and dismissals

TENURE CATEGORY (MONTHS)	CONTROL GROUP TURNOVER RATE	EXPERIMENTAL GROUP	
		AVERAGE MONTHLY FORCE SIZE	PREDICTED RESIGNATIONS AND DISMISSALS
A	B	C	D
0–6	47.6%	1.4	0.67
6–12	23.3	2.2	0.51
12–18	35.7	3.6	1.29
18–30	13.2	6.1	0.81
30–42	12.3	6.1	0.75
42–60	27.8	6.4	1.78
60–96	17.5	3.6	0.63
Total	21.2%	29.4	6.44

judge the child care center to have had a slightly beneficial effect on turnover.

If it appears odd that the control group, averaging 37.8 people, is larger than the experimental group, averaging 29.4 employees, this is because parents naturally were allowed to enroll or withdraw their children from the center at will throughout the period covered. Each time a new enrollment occurred, the parent automatically was added to the experimental group; each time a withdrawal took place, the parent was deleted from the experimental group thenceforth. The control group, on the other hand, was repeatedly augmented by matching an employee to the parent of each child newly enrolled in the center, but was not correspondingly diminished when a child was withdrawn. It may be questioned whether such a procedure is methodologically sound, but it accounts at any rate for the discrepancy in average size between the two groups.

TABLE 5(c)
Illustrative cost benefit analysis

		EXPERIMENTAL GROUP			
TENURE CATEGORY (MONTHS)	PROTO-TYPICAL INVEST-MENT LOST	PRE-DICTED Rs AND Ds	PREDICTED INVEST-MENT LOST	ACTUAL INVEST-MENT LOST	COST/BENEFIT
A	B	C	D	E	F
0–6	$5,229	0.67	$ 3,503	$ 5,229	($1,726)
6–12	6,273	0.51	3,199	6,273	(3,074)
12–18	4,367	1.29	5,633	4,367	1,266
18–30	2,733	0.81	2,214	0	2,214
30–42	1,245	0.75	934	1,245	(311)
42–60	492	1.78	876	492	384
60–96	0	0.63	0	0	0
Total	—	6.44	$16,359	$17,606	($1,247)

Application of FLCA.   FLCA now may be applied to the data as follows. Assuming that the results for the control group exemplify the natural order of affairs in the absence of a child care center, and assuming further that the center had no impact on turnover during the period in question, we would expect the turnover rates by tenure category to be the same for the experimental group as for the control group. This expectation permits an *ex post facto* "prediction" of the number of resignations and dismissals the experimental group would have experienced if the child care center had not existed. The calculations are shown in Table 5(b).

Columns A, B, and C of the table are copied from Table 5(a). Column D is obtained by multiplying columns B and C and dividing by 100. It is simply a matter of applying the control-group turnover rates to the experimental-group average monthly force sizes. As the bottom row indicates, a total of 6.43 resignations and dismissals are predicted for the experimental group, as against the five that actually took place. By subtraction, the net saving in turnover due to the child care center is evidently 1.43 Service Representative replacements per year.

Table 5(c) presents the information necessary to translate this saving into dollars. Column B shows the amount of investment lost on a solitary instance of turnover within each tenure category, i.e., the prototypical case. Column C is copied from Table 5(b). Column D is the product of columns B and C — in the first row of column D, e.g., if one case of turnover costs $5229, then two-thirds of a turnover costs $3503 (0.67 × $5229). The total for column D is the amount of investment that would have been lost if the experimental group had turned over at exactly the control group rates, whereas column E is the investment lost on the five experimental group resignations and dismissals that actually did take place.

Column F, the difference between D and E, supplies the answer, finally, to the cost-benefit question. Not curiously — in light of the fact that the data were tampered with by the writer — the cost figures contradict the turnover statistics. Despite the lower rate of turnover in the experimental group, the child care center shows a cost disadvantage for the year of $1247. The reason, of course, is that resignations and dismissals in the control group tended to occur at later stages of job tenure than in the experimental group, meaning that more investment had been previously amortized. This shows that conversion of turnover data to dollars via FLCA can do more than lend increased precision to an analysis; under some circumstances it can cast the findings in an opposite light.

Plainly, no faith could be placed in the statistical reliability of the above analysis even if the data were genuine. The numbers of people involved are so small that a single instance of turnover in either the experimental or control group could reverse the verdict. In practice, a program of this nature would have to be tracked for several years, not merely to establish reliable trends, but to ensure that the outcomes observed are not products of extraneous influences such as "Hawthorne effect." Moreover, to bring the cost-benefit analysis to completion, any savings ultimately identified as emanating from the program would have to be balanced against the added costs incurred in initiating and operating the program. No such costs are considered in the present example.

There are occasions where it is more convenient, or more logical, to do a FLCA cost-benefit analysis using retention, or survival, rates instead of turnover rates within tenure categories.[6] The computations are somewhat different, but the basic logic is the same. Examples are available but not included here.

Job mobility programs. Programs to stimulate job mobility in the form of transfers and promotions have become as much a focus of concern in American business nowadays as programs to cut down work-force losses. In addition to their other merits, mobility programs also may have a favorable long-term effect on resignations and dismissals. Hence, FLCA has a role to play in assessing their cost beneficialness, too. However, rather than take the space to explain in full how FLCA fits into cost-benefit studies of mobility programs, I will limit the discussion to a sketch of the main ideas.

As already noted, whenever anyone is transferred or promoted, FLCA transfers the unexpired remainder of the investment in the employee to an account associated with the new job. The manager of this account, i.e., the "receiving" manager, thus is required to absorb not only the expense of carrying the transferred investment, i.e., the amortization, but also the carrying charges on whatever further investment must be made to enable the employee to master the new job. From the viewpoint of the receiving manager, this is the debit side of the ledger. In exchange, the receiving manager is accorded two potential economic benefits.

One prospective benefit is that the transferee/promotee may learn the new job faster than would a replacement hired from outside the business, thus reducing the new investment to be added and, *ergo,* the subsequent carrying charges on this investment. The other possible benefit is that the transferee/

promotee will constitute a smaller force-loss risk than would an outside hire. If so, the lower probability of resignation and dismissal will manifest itself in longer job tenure and, in turn, a slower rate of amortization. To determine the net outcome from the perspective of the receiving manager, this pair of benefits then can be weighed against the cost disadvantage of assuming the transferred initial investment.

Let us suppose the above comparison proves favorable. The former, or "sending," manager now is faced with replacing the transferred or promoted worker. Barring unusual circumstances, there is scarcely any way this replacement can be cost-beneficial. The manager must assume carrying charges on the replacement employee that are greater than before, both because the new investment exceeds the transferred investment and because the risk of turnover is higher for the replacement employee than for the employee replaced. The measure of the cost disadvantage to the sending manager is the difference between the new and old carrying charges.

Finally, to arrive at a cost-benefit judgment from the standpoint of the transaction as a whole, the cost disadvantage realized by the sending manager must be deducted from the benefit attained by the receiving manager. The difference tells the story.

To conduct an FLCA cost-benefit study of a mobility program along the lines described, it is necessary to measure differentials in on-job learning costs and turnover probabilities as between transferred and promoted employees, on the one side, and outside hires, on the other. This poses a formidable obstacle in the case of newly established programs, since it may take months to accumulate data for calculation of differential costs for replacement components such as efficiency recovery and extra supervision, and years to amass data for computation of differential turnover probabilities. There seems to be no way of overcoming this problem except by guessing values for the parameters, then adjusting the guesses as empirical evidence builds up.

It may be observed incidentally that the question of differential on-job learning costs and turnover probabilities has far-reaching implications, not just for FLCA, but for manpower planning, training, and selection and placement of employees generally. It seems an issue worth devoting research attention to, even if it does take time for the final answers to forthcome.

Miscellaneous Applications

Numerous additional applications of FLCA are anticipated beyond those above, but considerations of space preclude giving them more than brief mention. Data on differential training costs and turnover probabilities can assist, for instance, in deciding whether to promote from within or hire from without. Knowledge of replacement costs can aid likewise in deciding whether to lay off employees when sales go down or to retain them on the payroll until sales rise again.[7] Improved understanding of the effects of initial training on the costs of on-job learning can be helpful in measuring the effectiveness of training and finding ways to make it better. To stretch the imagination a bit, it is not inconceivable that retirement programs and other employee benefits could be rationalized better by knowing more about turnover costs and what would happen to these costs as a result of changes in company policy.

FORCE-LOSS COST ANALYSIS METHODS

Cost Variation

No finding throughout FLCA's history has more persistently intruded itself on our awareness than the great diversity in replacement costs from one organizational unit to another. In one study, for instance, we found that the cost of hiring employees to perform a specified job in a given work location varied across different employment offices by a factor of four. In other words, of two people hired the same day and working side by side at the same occupation, one might cost four times as much to employ as the other. In the same study we found the cost of extra supervision for a given job in two ostensibly similar work locations to differ by over $1750. In various investigations we have found the replacement cost for the job of Directory Assistance Operator to range from $1259 to $6656.

Although FLCA uses group-accounting methods for all employees within a work location, we have studied differential costs by individual employee enough to suspect that the variation among people may be just as spectacular as that among organizational units. Mentioned earlier, for example, was a $578 difference in efficiency recovery cost between high producing and low producing telephone operators.

Since variation, not uniformity, in cost appears to be the keynote of FLCA, we have not attempted to develop average costs for any occupation; and my inclination is to be cautious, if not skeptical, about average costs cited by anyone else. We recommend, instead, that cost data be derived locally for every organizational unit in which FLCA is applied.

It is recognized that such a stance is partially self-defeating in that it magnifies the task of implementation. Under accommodating conditions it takes only a few man-weeks to generate the requisite cost data for a given organizational unit, but there are thousands of organizational units in the Bell Telephone System. All the same, I have sufficient confidence in the power and utility, if not to say inevitability, of FLCA to believe that the added labor is justified and the recommendation reasonable. The alternative is to use global averages, which experience tells us would render the results largely meaningless.

The Procedural Guide

To support local development of cost data, we have prepared a manual called the *Force-Loss Cost Analysis Procedural Guide,* which is little more than an expanded version of the procedural guide prepared and employed in one of our earliest FLCA studies. The *Guide* describes the derivation of every cost component considered in that study, including the calculations performed and the reference materials used. An illustrative page from the *Guide* appears in Fig. 2.

The occupation reviewed in the study illustrated by Fig. 2 is that of telephone operator. The page displayed outlines the com-

1.3305 ORANGE TRAFFIC DISTRICT MANAGER OVERHEAD LOADING RATE

Description

Wages and Salaries:
Staff: Salaries of the Orange District Traffic Manager,
his direct reporting subordinate managers, and his District
Office support personnel;
Wage Base: Total District Central Office operator and
clerical salaries. The assumption is made that this managerial
group's functions are fully allocable to the Central Office
operations people in proportion to their respective salaries.

Bills and Vouchers: Miscellaneous expenses of the Traffic
Manager.

Exceptions: None.

Data Sources

The District Traffic Manager group salaries were obtained
from the Essex Area Traffic Supervisor's office (Ref. R11).

For the wage base, the Essex Area Traffic Budget worksheet
(showing Central Office operating and clerical salaries,
accounts 624-11 and 624-321 by Central Offices) was developed
with the Operations Supervisor-Budgets (Ref. R12).

Factor

The factor, applicable to any Orange District Central Office
operating or clerical employee's salary, is derived from the
following computation (based on the study period Jan-Dec 1971):

$$\frac{\text{Salaries of District Office Manager group}}{\text{Salaries of Orange Central Office operating and clerical}} =$$

$$\frac{\$74,964}{\$2,453,016} = .0306 = 3.06\%$$

Recommendations

See Section 1.3302.

Fig. 2. *Sample page from the FLCA* Procedural Guide, *illustrating
the documentation of cost computations.*

putation of an overhead loading rate which is applied to operator wages elsewhere in the *Guide* in order to compute the costs of initial training and on-job learning. The technical content is not important; the figure is presented only to show how the calculation is explained and how cross-references are provided to supporting documents. This makes the loading rate auditable and facilitates periodic updating of the information reported.

Although the data contained in the *Guide* cannot be generalized beyond the locality where they were derived, we feel that the procedures followed are sufficiently general to enable any organization in the Bell System to use the *Guide* as a pattern for generating its own local costs and preparing its own manual.

Derived versus Estimated Costs

An obvious, natural way to generate replacement costs is to base them on estimates obtained from supervisors. This approach is doubly appealing because of its economy, and because operating managers generally are disinclined to question the resultant data. For purposes of FLCA, however, we have adopted the position that supervisory estimates are acceptable only if validity studies show such judgments to accord well with objective measurements. Unfortunately, the evidence so far available on this issue has not been encouraging.

Among the first FLCA studies undertaken was to compare supervisory estimates with empirical observations of the output quantity of telephone operators. Observations of the output quantity of individual operators are made by supervisors periodically. For purposes of this study, the outcome of observation was a raw count of the number of telephone calls per hour handled by each operator, averaged over several nonconsecutive hours.

Figure 3 contains two plots of calls-handled-per-hour as a function of job tenure, i.e., proficiency acquisition curves. The solid curve is derived from averages of observations made by the supervisors in one directory assistance office over a period of nine months. The dashed curve is based on the responses of the same supervisors to a questionnaire asking for estimates of the

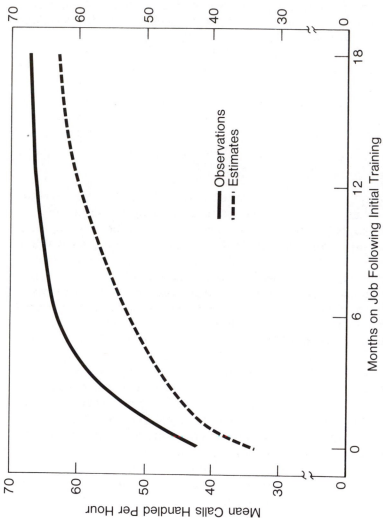

Fig. 3. *Proficiency acquisition curves for Directory Assistance Operators, comparing supervisory estimates with direct measurements of productivity.*

output quantity of an average operator having varying amounts of experience.[8] Because the number of new operators in an office at any one time is small, as is the number of supervisors (seven in this instance), both curves leave something to be desired in the way of statistical stability, but each gives the most representative indication of proficiency acquisition it is possible to obtain from the data sources employed.

It is evident without analysis that the supervisory estimates of the average rate of operator proficiency acquisition are more pessimistic than the empirical measurements would seem to warrant. In defense of the supervisors, it should be noted that this is a type of judgment they are rarely called on to make. Their powers of estimation no doubt would improve with practice. Also, Fig. 3 is an isolated finding from a single work location; it is possible that similar estimates by other groups of supervisors might strike closer to the mark.

Be that as it may, the discrepancy between the two curves is considerable. The empirical observations indicate that productivity reaches a virtual asymptote after six months on the job; the supervisory estimates show output quantity still rising sharply six months or more after that.

According to the figure, the average level of productivity after 18 months on the job is 67 calls per hour for the observational measurements, 63 calls per hour for the supervisory estimates. Using these numbers as respective operational definitions of job mastery, efficiency recovery cost for the observational data turns out to be $1084, and for the supervisory estimates, $2004. In other words, the managerial judgments yield a cost some 85 percent higher than the "actual."

If imperfection in managerial estimation such as the foregoing is a likely occurrence — and this must remain moot until more data become available — it further complicates the task of implementing FLCA. For not only must separate costs be established for each locality, some costs, especially the on-job learning costs, must be determined by means of a laborious data collection process. I happen to think that the information emanating from the data collection has value that more than repays the labor, but I may be prejudiced. It is not very difficult to understand how an operating manager might find FLCA, in its present form, too expensive for his tastes.

One area where we do permit the use of supervisory estimates, by the way, is in calculating subcosts for a larger component whose total cost is known already from independent sources. An example would be the selection phase of the employment process in which job applicants are tested, interviewed, given medical examinations, and subjected to other unavoidable indignities. Instead of separating the costs of testing, interviewing, and other subprocesses by means of time-and-motion study, we have been content to rely on supervisory judgment. Even if these judgments are wrong, other data still provide an accurate picture of the cost of the employment process as a whole.

The Standard of Job Mastery

One of the rules of FLCA, as earlier observed, is that investment ceases when job mastery is attained. Though straightforward enough intuitively, this is a hard concept to operationalize as there are innumerable ways of defining job mastery. These range everywhere from rate-of-return analysis through joint target setting to arbitrary managerial fiat.

To date in FLCA we have chosen to define mastery in terms of productivity, or speed of performance, rather than quality of workmanship. Also, we have elected to fix the requisite level of mastery for terminating investment accrual at the average level of productivity displayed by the experienced employees in any work group. This provides a working definition that is adequate for rough and tumble implementation, but is far from satisfactory theoretically. The problems inherent in such an approach have been outlined elsewhere and need not be dwelled on here.[9] One type of problem can be quickly illustrated, however, by looking again to Fig. 3.

The ordinates for the upper (solid) curve in Fig. 3 corresponding to 6, 12, and 18 months' job experience are, respectively, 63, 66, and 67 calls per hour. Statistically, these values are not significantly different, which suggests that the cut off point could be set, to suit the convenience of the analyst, anywhere from six months onward. Reinforcing this view is the finding, not depicted in the figure, that the average for operators in the same office with over two years' experience is 65 calls per hour. If the data were perfectly reliable, therefore, the cutoff should be set somewhere between six and twelve months.

But the data are not perfectly reliable. As a matter of fact, the standard error of the experienced operator average is 0.5 calls per hour, meaning that we can be confident only that the true average is somewhere between 63.5 and 66.5 calls per hour (i.e., within three standard errors of the 65 calls-per-hour average). Consequently, the cut off cannot be established with any degree of certainty within six months or so one way or the other.

Noting how the curve flattens after six months' experience, it may seem that it is academic where the cut off is made since subsequent on-job learning is negligible. Surprisingly, however, it appears to matter a good deal. If the cut off is fixed at six months, efficiency recovery cost is $632; if at twelve months, efficiency recovery cost is $933, or 48 percent larger. Thus on-job costs can be very sensitive to small variations in the method of calculation. We need to find a way to set standards on job mastery that will eliminate this area of fuzziness from FLCA. The matter is open to suggestion.

Overhead Loading Rates

In FLCA, miscellaneous costs of operating the business are allocated to direct-labor wages and salaries as overhead loadings. A telephone installer, for instance, operates a truck; in deriving replacement costs for this job, the carrying charges on the truck are loaded onto the installer's pay. As a result of this approach, overhead rates of 150 percent and more are not uncommon in FLCA. An example of the rates computed in one locality for the job of Employment Interviewer appears in Table 6. The Employment Interviewer's loaded wages come into play in figuring the hiring costs for other occupational groups.

TABLE 6
Illustrative overhead loading rates for
employment interviewers

BURDENING FACTOR	RATE (%)
General overhead:	
General expense	6.4%
Relief and pensions	18.3
Social security	5.0
Supervision and staff:	
Salaries and expenses:	
Territory staff	5.9
Staff supervisor, employment	9.9
Employment office supervisor	11.2
Facilities:	
Territory staff:	0.1
Staff supervisor, employment	0.7
District employment office	29.5
Total	87.0%

Although extensive philosophizing preceded formulation of
the overhead loading rules, and we believe they have much to be
said in their behalf, we recognize their controversiality and try to
abstain from arguments as to their propriety. Instead, we prag-
matically enumerate all the constituent parts of the total loading
rate, as in Table 6, then describe each part fully in the *Procedural
Guide,* as in Fig. 2. Anyone who disagrees with the procedure is
now free to reconstruct the rates in whatever manner he wishes.

Amortization

At the start of the FLCA research project we labored in the belief that amortization was among the commandments brought down from the mountain by Moses. As a result, considerable energy was expended studying alternate methods of amortization in an effort to understand their consequences and to find the most defensible approach to employ.[10] More recently, we have come to recognize that although amortization is a useful consideration in measuring past results, investment accumulated (disregarding amortization) is the critical factor in making decisions about the future. To know what fraction of a previous investment has been written off the books is of little help in deciding how to spend current funds.[11] From the point of view of FLCA as a decision-making tool, therefore, the choice of amortization method may be comparatively immaterial.

In any case, the guiding principle of amortization in FLCA is to depreciate investment over the expected future job tenure of the individual worker, recognizing that the probable future tenure of any employee is a variable depending heavily on tenure acquired to date. This is in contrast to depreciating investment for everybody over the same fixed interval. Although many computational options are available — such as, e.g., declining balance — FLCA by and large has adhered to the straight-line method. Thus the amortization procedure is not dissimilar to that used in the celebrated human resource accounting program of the R.G. Barry Company.[12,13] There are, however, one or two differences of detail that may be worth reviewing.

Because of generally higher turnover among short-service employees, the longer anyone has stayed on a job, the longer he can be expected to remain in the future (within limits). A prediction of future job tenure, given a specified current tenure, can be obtained by constructing a contingency table from past experience exactly the way an actuary builds a table of life expectancies. An example appears in Table 7.

Table 7 is derived from some 373 instances of Service Representative turnover arising from all causes (i.e., resignation, dis-

TABLE 7
Service representative dynamic average tenure, one city, July 1969 to June 1971

MONTHS OF CURRENT TENURE		MONTHS OF TENURE EXPECTED	
MORE THAN:	NOT MORE THAN:	DYNAMIC AVERAGE	ANTICIPATED REMAINING
0 mos.	1 mo.	29 mos.	29 mos.
1	2	30	29
2	3	32	30
3	4	36	33
4	5	38	34
5	6	41	36
6	7	43	37
7	8	45	38
8	9	47	39
9	10	48	39
10	11	50	40
11	12	52	41
12	15	54	40
15	18	60	43
18	21	65	45
21	24	69	46
24	30	73	46
30	36	87	54
36	42	96	57
42	48	104	59
48	60	121	67
60	72	142	76
72	120	173	97
120	180	269	119
300	Retirement	468	108

missal, transfer, promotion, extended leave of absence, retirement, and death) in one major city during a two-year base period. To illustrate how the table is read, the fifth line predicts that the average Service Representative having now between four and five months of job tenure will survive in the job a total of 38 months, or 34 months more than the four-plus months already completed. For the prediction of total tenure, given current tenure, we have coined the name "dynamic average tenure."

The right-most column, anticipated remaining tenure, contains the intervals required for straight-line amortization. For a Service Representative in this particular city, the investment remaining at the end of five months would be depreciated by the fraction 1/34th, at the end of six months by the fraction 1/36th, at the end of seven months by the fraction 1/37th, and so forth. By the time a Service Representative has achieved ten years' service (120 months), the amortization interval has stretched to nearly 10 years (119 months), so the monthly write-off becomes 1/119th of whatever investment remains.

The R.G. Barry Company's amortization procedure is similar in spirit to the above, but involves an adjustment in net investment, that FLCA does not include, following each accounting period. A detailed comparison of the two methods is reported elsewhere.[10]

Intuitively, one expects the amount of investment amortized at the end of any accounting period to bear some relation to the value received from the investment during the period. Accordingly, since new employees are less productive usually than experienced workers, proportionate reductions are made in amortization rates during the period of proficiency acquisition. If the average employee with a given length of tenure is, say, 75 percent productive, the normal straight-line depreciation rate for that tenure category is diminished by an amount proportional to $100\% - 75\% = 25\%$. This is a refinement which we believe may be original with FLCA and is aimed at making the amortization process more meaningful to operating managers. It allows one to think of amortization as hinging not only on projected job tenure, but on level of productivity as well. The computational details are spelled out in the report on amortization cited before.[10]

THE FUTURE OF FORCE-LOSS COST ANALYSIS

The future of force-loss cost analysis, like that of every technological innovation, depends on the demand that develops for the product. This demand will rest, in turn, on three primary considerations.

The first is the extent to which managerial concern continues to be manifested over the high costs of force loss which are now a fact of business life. In light of recent worldwide economic developments, it seems possible that many countries may be headed for a buyer's market in personnel that could endure longer than anyone would like to think. In that event, it would be natural for interest in force-loss costs to abate, thereby diminishing the demand for FLCA for some time to come. Even so, there still would exist more than enough useful applications of FLCA, in my opinion, to justify its continued development and implementation in the short run. Whether others will share this view, only time can tell.

A closely allied consideration in predicting demand for FLCA is the degree to which managerial concern is sustained over the cost-effectiveness of policies and programs designed to increase the upward mobility of employees. In the short run, again, a buyer's market could weaken this concern materially. However, it is scarcely conceivable that the pressure for occupational mobility that has been building for generations can be capped permanently by oil embargoes or any similarly transient perturbations of the economy.

The third consideration is the extent to which interest will grow in rational management of the personnel process, particularly aspects of manpower planning related to internal movement and replacement of employees. Much of our original thinking about FLCA was predicated on the assumption that this is where the greatest demand would emerge, and the earliest examples of FLCA dealt with it as a day-to-day management tool. I retain the faith that scientific manpower management is the iris through which FLCA one day will shine forth in transcendent glory, but sober judgment must acknowledge that the millennium is not yet here. How rapidly business managers will move to adopt more rational decision-making methods concerning human resources is anybody's guess.

In view of the foregoing imponderables, it is difficult to foresee what the future holds in store for FLCA. Whatever happens, we plan to continue developmental research on various issues remaining still unclear.

Complexity of FLCA

Experience has proved that many operating managers, though by no means all, find FLCA hard to understand. I am not certain what causes the difficulty. Some of the details are, to be sure, a bit complicated. But the fundamental ideas seem simple and straightforward. Conceptually, FLCA is little more than a translation of traditional cost accounting principles to fit a nontraditional subject matter. One would imagine that business managers would find such a translation both easy to grasp and welcome. More investigation needs to be done to discover the source of the communication problem.

Accountants, on the other hand, not only have little trouble understanding FLCA, they regard most of it as elementary. Partly for this reason, and partly because FLCA is essentially an accounting discipline anyway, I believe it vital that the basic mechanics — collection of data, calculation of results, manipulation of accounts, etc. — be placed under the supervision of professional accountants rather than under the direction of operating staffs, personnel staffs, or behavioral scientists. By doing so, what otherwise can appear a complex, frustrating data processing operation gets transformed into something routine and mundane. This recommendation will seem obvious and trivial to accountants, of course, but it may be less so to others who, in the absence of an explicit statement, may not appreciate that there is anything accountants are good for.

Technical Problems

A number of technical problems remain to be resolved. Some of these, such as fixing a cut off point for investment accrual, have been mentioned. Another is measurement of proficiency acquisition rates, which requires accurate, reliable information about the productivity levels of individual employees. This information is difficult enough to come by for any job, let alone jobs such as chauffeur or secretary where the criteria of productivity are nebulous. Still another problem is measurement of the cost of extra supervision afforded new employees. Since very often there are no extant sources from which this cost can be computed, it is frequently necessary to institute an odious, new record-keeping procedure.

Technical problems like these are not, however, a prohibitive impediment to FLCA. Where research cannot supply answers to unresolved issues, common sense and guile can find temporary solutions that will do until better ones come along. FLCA, like every new technology, has growing pains, but these should disappear with maturity and experience.

REFERENCES

Note: The documents listed below as company proprietary are available for limited distribution to qualified requesters. Address requests to H.W. Gustafson, American Telephone and Telegraph Company, 1776 On The Green, Room 4A15, Morristown, New Jersey, 07960.

[1] Bassett, G.A. (1972). Employee Turnover Measurement and Human Resources Accounting. *Human Resource Management,* Fall, 21–30.

[2] Flamholtz, E.G. (1973). Human Resources Accounting: Measuring Positional Replacement Costs. *Human Resource Management,* Spring, 8–16.

[3] Gaudet, F.J. (1960). *Labor Turnover: Calculation and Cost.* (New York: American Management Association, Research Study) 39.

[4] *Force-Loss Cost Analysis Report.* AT&T Company, June 1972. (Company proprietary.)

[5]*Acquisition of Proficiency by Directory Assistance Operators Following a Readiness Training Program.* AT&T Company, June 1972. (Company proprietary.) Report prepared under contract by SERCO, Washington, D.C.

[6]Van Der Merwe, R., and Miller, S. (1971). The Measurement of Labour Turnover. *Human Relations* **24**:233–52.

[7] Alexander, M.O. Investments in People. *Canadian Chartered Accountant,* July 1971, 38–45.

[8]*Comparative Analysis of Operator Performance Measures.* AT&T Company, February 1973. (Company proprietary.) Report prepared under contract by SERCO, Washington, D.C.

[9]Gustafson, H.W. (1973). Special Treatment for Special People: A Minority Report on the Training of Minorities. *Business Perspectives* **9**:2–11.

[10]*Amortization Methods as Applied to Force-Loss Cost Analysis.* AT&T Company, June 1972. (Company proprietary.) Report prepared under contract by Brenner Associates, New Brunswick, N.J.

[11]Grant, E.L., and Ireson, W.G. *Principles of Engineering Economy,* 4th ed. (New York: Ronald Press, 1960).

[12]Brummet, R.L., Pyle, W.C., and Flamholtz, E.G. (1969). Human Resource Accounting in Industry. *Personnel Administration* **32**:34–46.

[13]Pyle, W.C. (1970). Monitoring Human Resources — 'On Line'. *Michigan Business Review* **22**:19–32.

Bibliography

Abram, T.G. (1979). Overview of the uniform selection guidelines: Pitfalls for the unwary employer. *Industrial Relations Research Association Proceedings* April: 495–502.

Armknecht, P.A., and Early, J.F. (1972). Quits in manufacturing: A study of their causes. *Monthly Labor Review* **95**: 31–37.

Arvey. R.D. (1979). *Fairness in Selecting Employees.* Reading, Mass.: Addison-Wesley.

Bailyn, L. (1970). Career and family orientations of husbands and wives in relation to marital happiness. *Human Relations* **23**: 97–113.

Baron, J.M., and McCafferty, S. (1977). Job search, labor supply and the quit decision: Theory and endurance. *American Economic Review* **67**: September, 683–91.

Bartol, K.M. (1979). Professionalism as a predictor of organizational commitment, role stress, and turnover: A multidimensional approach. *Academy of Management Journal* **22**: 815–21.

Bassett, G.A. (1972). Employee turnover measurement and human resources accounting. *Human Resource Management* Fall: 21–30.

——— (1967). *A Study of Factors Associated with Turnover of Exempt Personnel.* Crotonville: Personnel and Industrial Relations Services. General Electric.

Becker, G.S. (1964). *Human Capital.* New York: Columbia University Press.

Bezanson, A. (1928). The advantages of labor turnover: An illustrative case. *Quarterly Journal of Economics* **42**: 3, 450–64.

Blau, P.M. (1973). *The Organization of Academic Work.* New York: Wiley.

Blau, P.M.; Gustad, J.W.; Jessor, R.; Parnes, H.S.; and Wilcox, R.C. (1956). Occupational choice: A conceptual framework. *Industrial and Labor Relations Review* **8**: 531–43.

Block, F.E. (1979). Labor turnover in U.S. manufacturing industries. *The Journal of Human Resources* **14**: 236–46.

Bluedorn, A.C. (1981). The theories of turnover. In S. Bacharach (ed.), *Perspectives in Sociology: Theory and Research.* Greenwich, Conn.: JAI Press.

——— (1980). A unified model of turnover from organizations. Paper presented at the 40th Annual meeting of the Academy of Management, Detroit, August.

——— (1978). A taxonomy of turnover. *Academy of Management Review,* 3 July, 647–51.

Borjas, G.J. (1979). Job satisfaction, wages, and unions. *The Journal of Human Resources* **14**: 21–40.

Borman, W.C. (1978). Exploring the upper limits of reliability and validity in job performance ratings. *Journal of Applied Psychology* **63**: 135–44.

Brayfield, A.H., and Rothe, H.F. (1951). An index of job satisfaction. *Journal of Applied Psychology* **35**: 307–11.

Brayfield, A.H., and Crockett, W.H. (1955). Employee attitudes and employee performance. *Psychological Bulletin* **52**: 396–424.

Brummet, R.L.; Pyle, W.C.; and Flamholtz, E. (1969). Human resources accounting in industry. *Personnel Administration* July–August.

Bureau of National Affairs (1981). *BNA's Quarterly Report on Job Absence and Turnover.* Washington, D.C.: Bureau of National Affairs, March.

Burke, R.J., and Wilcox, D.S. (1972). Absenteeism and turnover among female telephone operators. *Personnel Psychology* **25**: 639–48.

Burton, J.F., and Parker, J.E. (1969). Interindustry variation in voluntary labor mobility. *Industrial and Labor Relations Review,* January, **22**: 199–216.

Byrt, W.J. (1957). Methods of measuring labor turnover. *Personnel Practices Bulletin* **13**: 6–14.

Canfield, G.W. (1959). How to compute your labor turnover costs. *Personnel Journal* **37**: 413–17.

Carey, M.L. (1976). Revised occupational projections to 1985. *Monthly Labor Review,* November, 10–22.

Cascio, W.F. (1976). Turnover, biographical data, and fair employment practice. *Journal of Applied Psychology* **61**: 576–80.

Cawsey, T.F., and Wedley, W.C. (1979). Labor turnover costs: Measurement and control. *Personnel Journal* 90–5, 212.

Cawsey, T.F., and Richardson, P. (1975). Turnover can be managed. *Business Quarterly,* Winter, 57–63.

Chaplin, D. (1968). Labor turnover in the Peruvian textile industry. *British Journal of Industrial Relations* **6**: 58–78.

Conference Board (1972). *Salesmen: Turnover in Early Employment.* New York: Conference Board.

Coverdale, S.H., and Terborg, J.R. (1980). A re-examination of the Mobley, Horner, and Hollingsworth model of turnover: A useful replication. Paper presented at the 40th Annual Meeting of the Academy of Management, Detroit, August.

Cramer, K.D. (1978). An evaluation of the psychological climate process in relation to individual and organizational effectiveness. *Dissertation Abstracts International* **39**: 1525.

Dachler, H.P., and Mobley, W.H. (1973). Construct validation of an instrumentality expectancy task-goal model of work motivation. Some theoretical boundary conditions. *Journal of*

Applied Psychology **58**: 397—418.

Dalton, D.R., and Todor, W.D. (1979). Turnover turned over: An expanded and positive perspective. *Academy of Management Review* **4**: 225—35.

Dalton, D.R.; Todor, W.D.; and Krackhardt, D.M. (1982). Turnover overstated: The functional taxonomy. *Academy of Management Review,* in press.

Dansereau, F., Jr.; Cashman, J.; and Graen, G. (1974). Expectancy as a moderator of the relationship between job attitudes and turnover. *Journal of Applied Psychology* **59**: 228—29.

Decker, P.J., and Cornelius, E.T., III. (1979). A note on recruiting sources and job survival rates. *Journal of Applied Psychology* **64**: 463—64.

DeCotiis, T.A., and Petit, A. (1978). The performance appraisal process: A model and some testable propositions. *Academy of Management Review* **21**:635—46.

Douglas, P.H. (1918). The problem of labor turnover. *American Economic Review* **8**: 306—16.

Drucker, P.F. (1980). *Managing in Turbulent Times.* New York: Harper and Row.

Dubin, R.; Champoux, J.; and Porter, L. (1975). Central life interests and organizational commitment of blue collar and clerical workers. *Administrative Science Quarterly* **20**: 411—21.

Dunham, R.B., and Smith, F.J. (1979). *Organizational Surveys: An Internal Assessment of Organizational Health.* Glenview, Illinois: Scott, Foresman and Company.

Dunnette, M.D.; Arvey, R.D.; and Banas, P.A. (1973). Why do they leave? *Personnel* **50**: 25—38.

Dyer, L.; Schwab, D.P.; and Fossum, J.A. (1978). Impacts of pay on employee behaviors and attitudes: An update. *Personnel Administrator* **23**: 51—7.

Ekpo-Ufot, A. (1976). Self-perceived abilities relevant in the task (SPART): A potential predictor of labor turnover in an industrial work setting. *Personnel Psychology* **29**: 405—16.

Endicott, F.S. (1978). *The Endicott Report 1979.* Evanston, Illinois: Northwestern University.

Equal Employment Opportunity Commission, Civil Service Commission, Department of Labor, Department of Justice (1978). Uniform guidelines on employee selection procedures. *Federal Register* **43**: August 25, 28290.

——— (1979). Adoption of questions and answers to clarify and provide a common interpretation of uniform guidelines on employee selection. *Federal Register* **44**: March 2, 11995.

——— (1980). Adoption of additional questions and answers to clarify and provide a common interpretation of the uniform guidelines on employee selection. *Federal Register* **45**: May 2, 29530.

Farr, J.L.; O'Leary, B.S.; and Bartlett, C.J. (1973). Effect of work sample test upon self-selection and turnover of job applicants. *Journal of Applied Psychology* **58**: 283–85.

Federico, J.M.; Federico, P.; and Lundquist, G.W. (1976). Predicting women's turnover as a function of extent of met salary expectations and biodemographic data. *Personnel Psychology* **29**: 559–66.

Fishbein, M., and Ajzen, I. (1975). *Belief, Attitudes, Intention, and Behavior.* Reading, Mass.: Addison-Wesley.

Flamholtz, E. (1974). *Human Resources Accounting.* Encino, California: Dickenson Publishing.

——— (1973). Human resource accounting: Measuring positional replacement costs. *Human Resource Management,* Spring.

Flanagan, R.J. (1978). Discrimination theory, labor turnover, and racial unemployment differentials. *The Journal of Human Resources* **13**: 187–205.

Fleishman, E.A., and Harris, E.F. (1962). Patterns of leadership behavior related to employee grievances and turnover. *Personnel Psychology* **15**: 43–56.

Flowers, V.S., and Hughes, C.L. (1973). Why employees stay. *Harvard Business Review,* July–August, 49–60.

Forrest, C.R.; Cummings, L.L.; and Johnson, A.C. (1977). Organizational participation: A critique and model. *Academy of Management Review* 2: 586–601.

Fossum, J.A.; Keaveny, T.J.; and Jackson, J.H. (1977). Expressed willingness to change jobs examined within the March and Simon participation framework. Laramie, WY: Institute for Polling Research, Research Paper 210.

Frantzreb, R. (1977). Controlling turnover. *Manpower Planning* 1: May, 1.

Fry, F.L. (1973). A behavioral analysis of economic variables affecting turnover. *Journal of Behavioral Economics* 2: 247–95.

Gannon, M.J. (1971). Sources of referral and employee turnover. *Journal of Applied Psychology* **55**: 226–28.

Gaudet, F.J. (1960). *Labor Turnover: Calculation and Cost.* New York: American Management Association, Research Study 39.

Gellerman, S.W. (1974). In praise of those who leave. *The Conference Board Record* **11**: 35–40.

Gillet, B., and Schwab, D.P. (1975). Convergent and discriminant validities of corresponding Job Descriptive Index and Minnesota Satisfaction Questionnaire scales. *Journal of Applied Psychology* **60**: 313–17.

Goodman, P.S.; Salipante, P.; and Paransky, H. (1973). Hiring, training, and retaining the hard core unemployed: A selected review. *Journal of Applied Psychology* **58**: 23–33.

Graen, G.B. (1976). Role-making processes within complex organizations. In M.D. Dunnette (ed.). *Handbook of Industrial and Organizational Psychology,* Chicago: Rand McNally.

Graen, G.B.; Orris, J.B.; and Johnson, T.W. (1973). Role assimilation processes in a complex organization. *Journal of Vocational Behavior* 3: 395–420.

Graen, G.B., and Ginsburgh, S. (1977). Job resignation as a function of role orientation and leader acceptance: A longitudinal investigation of organization assimilation. *Organizational Behavior and Human Performance* **19**: 1–17.

Gustafson, H.W. (1980). *Force-Loss Cost Analysis.* New York: American Telephone and Telegraph Co.

Hackman, J.R., and Oldham, G.R. (1975). Development of the job diagnostic survey. *Journal of Applied Psychology* **60**: 159–79.

Hall, D.T. (1976). *Careers in Organizations.* Pacific Palisades, Calif.: Goodyear Publishing.

Hellriegel, D., and White, G.E. (1973). Turnover of professionals in public accounting: A comparative analysis. *Personnel Psychology* **26**: 239–49.

Heneman, H.G., III, and Schwab, D.P. (1975). Work and rewards theory. In D. Yoder and H.G. Heneman, Jr. (eds.). *ASPA Handbook of Research and Industrial Relation.* Volume II, Motivation and Commitment. Washington, D.C. Bureau of National Affairs.

Herman, J.B., and Hulin, C.L. (1972). Studying organizational attitudes from individual and organizational frames of reference. *Organizational Behavior and Human Performance* **8**:84–108.

Herman, J.B.; Dunham, R.B.; and Hulin, C.L. (1975). Organizational structure, demographic characteristics and employee responses. *Organizational Behavior and Human Performance* **13**: 206–32.

Hill, J.M., and Trist, E.L. (1955). Changes in accidents and other absences with length of service: A further study of their incidence and relation to each other in an iron and steel works. *Human Relations* **8**: 121–52.

Hines, G.H. (1973). Achievement motivation, occupations, and labor turnover in New Zealand. *Journal of Applied Psychology* **59**:313–17.

Hinrichs, J.R. (1980). *Controlling Absenteeism and Turnover.* Scarsdale, N.Y.: Work in America Institute, Inc.

Holmes, R.A. (1980). What's ahead for personnel professionals in the 80's: Employers should begin mounting the offensive in discrimination suits. *Personnel Administrator* June, 33–7.

Hom, P.; Katerberg, R.; and Hulin, C.L. (1979). Comparative examination of three approaches to the prediction of turnover. *Journal of Applied Psychology* **64**: 280–90.

Horner, S.D. (1979). A field experimental study of affective, intentional, and behavioral effects of organizational entry expectations. Unpublished Ph.D. dissertation, Columbia, S.C.: University of South Carolina.

Horner, S.D.; Mobley, W.H.; and Meglino, B.M. (1979). An experimental evaluation of the effects of a realistic job preview on Marine recruit affect, intentions, and behavior. *ONR Technical Report* No. 9, Columbia, S.C.: Center for Management and Organizational Research, University of South Carolina.

Hrebiniak, L.G., and Alutto, J.A. (1972). Personal and role-related factors in the development of organizational commitment. *Administrative Science Quarterly* **17**: 555–73.

Huck, D.F., and Midlam, K.D. (1977). A model to analyze the cost of first term attrition in the Navy and Marine Corps. In W. Sinaiko (ed.) *First Term Enlisted Attrition.* Washington, D.C.: Smithsonian Institute Manpower Advisory Services.

Hulin, C.L. (1968). Effects of changes in job satisfaction levels on employee turnover. *Journal of Applied Psychology* **52**: 122–26.

——— (1979). Integration of economics and attitude/behavior models to predict and explain turnover. Paper presented at Annual meeting of the Academy of Management, Atlanta.

Hulin, C.L., and Blood, M.R. (1968). Job enlargement, individual differences and work responses. *Psychological Bulletin* **69**: 41–55.

Ilgen, D.R., and Seely, W. (1974). Realistic expectations as an aid in reducing voluntary resignations. *Journal of Applied Psychology* **59**: 452–55.

Information Science Incorporated (1980). *Expanded EEO Compliance System.* Montvale, N.J.: Information Science Incorporated.

Ingham, G. (1979). *Size of Industrial Organization and Worker Behavior.* Cambridge: Cambridge University Press.

Jeswald, T.A. (1973). The cost of absenteeism and turnover in a large organization. In W.C. Hamner and F.L. Schmidt (eds.). *Contemporary Problems in Personnel.* Chicago: St. Clair Press, 352–57.

Johns, G. (1978). Task moderators of the relationship between leadership style and subordinate responses. *Academy of Management Journal* **21**: 319–25.

Kahn, R.L.; Wolfe, D.N.; Quinn, R.P.; Snoek, J.D.; and Rosenthal, D.A. (1964). *Organizational Stress: Studies In Role Confict and Ambiguity.* New York: Wiley.

Karp, H.B., and Nickson, J.W., Jr. (1973). Motivator-hygiene deprivation as a predictor of job turnover. *Personnel Psychology* **26**: 377–84.

Kasarda. (1973). Turnover. *Sociological Quarterly* **14**: 350–58.

Kerr, S.; Von Glinow, M.A.; and Schriesheim, J. (1977). Issues in the style of "professionals" in organizations: The case of scientists and engineers. *Organizational Behavior and Human Performance* **18**: 329–45.

Koch, J.L., and Steers, R.M. (1978). Job attachment, satisfaction, and turnover among public sector employees. *Journal of Vocational Behavior* **12**: 119–28.

Krackhardt, D.; McKenna, J.; Porter, L.W.; and Steers, R.W. (1981). Supervisory behavior and employee turnover: A field experiment. *Academy of Management Journal* **24**: 249–59.

Kraut, A.I. (1975). Predicting turnover of employees from measured job attitudes. *Organizational Behavior and Human Performance* **13**: 233–43.

Landy, F.J., and Farr, J.L. (1980). Performance rating. *Psychological Bulletin* **87**: 72–107.

Latham, G.P., and Wexley, K.N. (1981). *Increasing Productivity Through Performance Appraisal.* Reading, Mass.: Addison-Wesley.

Lawler, E.E., III. (1971). *Pay and Organizational Effectiveness: A Psychological View.* New York: McGraw-Hill.

——— (1973). *Motivation in Work Organizations.* Monterey: Brooks-Cole.

——— (1981). *Pay and Organizational Development.* Reading, Mass.: Addison-Wesley.

Lawler, E.E., III; Kuleck, J.J.P.; Rhode, J.G.; and Sorenson, J.E. (1975). Job choice and past decision dissonance. *Organizational Behavior and Human Performance* **13**: 133–45.

Lawler, E.E., III, and Rhode, J.G. (1976). *Information and Control in Organizations.* Pacific Palisades, Calif.: Goodyear.

Lee, R., and Booth, J.M. (1974). A utility analysis of a weighted application blank designed to predict turnover for clerical employees. *Journal of Applied Psychology* **59**:516–18.

Lefkowitz, J., and Katz, M.L. (1969). The validity of exit interviews. *Personnel Psychology* **22**: 445–55.

Leviatan, U. (1978). Organizational effects of managerial turnover in kibbutz production branches. *Human Relations* **31**: 1001–18.

Ley, R. (1966). Labor turnover as a function of worker differences, work environment, and authoritarianism of foremen. *Journal of Applied Psychology* **50**: 497–500.

Likert, R. (1973). Human resource accounting: Building and assessing productive organizations, *Personnel* **50**: 8–24.

Likert, R., and Bowers, D.G. (1973). Improving the accuracy of P/L reports by estimating the change in dollar value of the human organization. *Michigan Business Review* **25**: 15–24.

Locke, E.A. (1969). What is a job satisfaction? *Organizational Behavior and Human Performance* **4**: 309–36.

——— (1975). Personnel attitudes and motivation. *Annual Review of Psychology* **25**: 457–80.

———(1976). The nature and consequences of job satisfaction. In M.D. Dunnette (ed.). *Handbook of Industrial Organizational Psychology.* Chicago: Rand McNally.

Lyons, T.F. (1972). Turnover and absenteeism: A review of relationship and shared correlates, *Personnel Psychology* **5**: 271–81.

Macy, B.A., and Mirvis, P.H. (1976). A methodology for assessment of quality of work and organizational effectiveness in behavioral economic terms. *Administrative Science Quarterly* **21**: 212–26.

Mangione, T.W. (1973). Turnover: Some psychological and demographic correlates. In R.P. Quinn and T.W. Mangione (eds.). *The 1969–1970 Survey of Working Conditions.* Ann Arbor: University of Michigan Survey Research Center.

March, J.G., and Simon, H.A. (1958). *Organizations.* New York: Wiley.

Marsh, R., and Mannari, H. (1977). Organizational commitment and turnover: A predictive study. *Administrative Science Quarterly* **22**: 57–75.

Martin, T.N.; Price, J.L.; and Mueller, C.W. (1981). Job performance and turnover. *Journal of Applied Psychology* **66**: 116–19.

Merchants and Manufacturing Association (1959). *Labor Turnover—Causes, Costs, and Methods of Control.* Los Angeles.

Miller, H.E.; Katerberg, R.; and Hulin, C.L. (1979). Evaluation of the Mobley, Horner, and Hollingsworth model of employee turnover. *Journal of Applied Psychology* **64**: 509–17.

Mirvis, P.H., and Lawler, E.E., III. (1977). Measuring the financial impact of employee attitudes. *Journal of Applied Pscyhology* **62**:1–18.

Mirvis, P.H., and Macy, B.A. (1976). Human resource accounting: A measurement perspective. *Academy of Management Review* **1**: 74–83.

Mischel, W. (1976). *Introduction to Personality.* New York: Holt, Rinehart, and Winston.

Mixon, J.W. (1978). The minimum wage and voluntary labor mobility. *Industrial and Labor Relations Review* **32**: 67–73.

Mobley, W.H. (1980). The uniform guidelines on employee selection procedures: A retreat from reason? *Business and Economic Review,* March, **26**:8–11.

——— (1974). Meeting government guidelines on testing and selection. *Personnel Administrator,* November, **19**: 42–50.

——— (1974). The link between MBO and merit compensation. *Personnel Journal* 423–27.

——— (1977). Intermediate linkages in the relationships between job satisfaction and employee turnover. *Journal of Applied Psychology* **62**: 237–40.

——— (1980). Utility analysis in turnover research. Atlanta: Southeastern Psychological Association, March.

——— (1982). Some unanswered questions in turnover and withdrawal research. *Academy of Management Review,* in press.

Mobley, W.H., and Hall, K.B. (1973). Application of human resources accounting to training evaluation and decision making. Ann Arbor: Human Resources Association, University of Michigan, W.C. Pyle, Director.

Mobley, W.H.; Horner, S.D.; and Hollingsworth, A.T. (1978). An evaluation of precursors of hospital employee turnover. *Journal of Applied Psychology* **63**:408–14.

Mobley, W.H.; Griffeth, R.W.; Hand, H.H.; and Meglino, B.M. (1979). Review and conceptual analysis of the employee turnover process. *Psychological Bulletin* **86**: 493–522.

Moffatt, G.W., and Hill, K. (1970). Labor turnover in Australia: A review of research. *Personnel Practice Bulletin* **26**: 142–49.

Morris, F.C., Jr. (1978). *Current Trends in the Use and Misuse of Statistics Employment Discrimination Litigation.* Washington: Equal Employment Advisory Council.

Mowday, R.T. (1981). Viewing turnover from the perspective of those who remain: The relationship of job attitudes to attributions of the cause of turnover. *Journal of Applied Psychology* **66**: 120–23.

Mowday, R.T.; Steers, R.M.; and Porter, L.W. (1978). *The Measurement of Organizational Commitment.* Eugene, Oregon: Graduate School of Management, University of Oregon, ONR Technical Report, No. 15.

Mowday, R.T.; Steers, R.M.; and Porter, L.W. (1979). The measurement of organizational commitment. *Journal of Vocational Behavior* **14**: 224–27.

Mowday, R.T.; Koberg, C.S.; and McArthur, A.W. (1980). The psychology of the withdrawal process: A cross-validation of Mobley's intermediate linkages model of turnover. Paper presented at the 40th Annual Meeting of the Academy of Management, Detroit.

Muchinsky, P.M. (1977). Employee absenteeism: A review of the literature. *Journal of Vocational Behavior* **10**: 316–40.

Muchinsky, P.M., and Tuttle, M.L. (1979). Employee turnover: An empirical and methodological assessment. *Journal of Vocational Behavior* **14**: 43–77.

Muchinsky, P.M., and Morrow, P.C. (1980). A multidimensional model of voluntary employee turnover. *Journal of Vocational Behavior* **17**: 263–90.

Myers, M.S., and Flowers, V.S. (1974). A framework for measuring human assets. *California Management Review* **16**:5–16.

Newman, J.E. (1974). Predicting absenteeism and turnover: A field comparison of Fishbein's model and traditional job attitude measures. *Journal of Applied Psychology* **59**: 610–15.

Neumann, S., and Seger, E. (1978). Human resources and corporate risk management. *Personnel Journal* **57**: 76–9.

Nollen, S.D. (1980). What is happening to flextime, flexitour, gliding time, the variable day? And permanent and part-time employment? And the four-day week? *Across the Board.* New York: The Conference Board, April, 6–21.

Opinion Research Corporation (1974). *Employee Relations Research.* Princeton: Opinion Research Corporation.

Parnes, H.S. (1970). Labor force participation and labor mobility. In G.G. Somers (ed.). *A Review of Industrial Relations Research,* 1, Industrial Relations Research Association, 1–78.

Parsons, D.O. (1977). Models of labor market turnover: A theoretical and empirical survey. In R.G. Elrenbery (ed.), *Research in Labor Economics,* Vol. 1, Greenwich, Conn.: JAI Press.

Pencavel, J.H. (1970). *An Analysis of Quit Rate in American Manufacturing Industry,* Princeton, Industrial Relations Section, Princeton University.

Peters, L.H.; Jackofsky, E.F.; and Salter, J.R. (1981). Predicting turnover: A comparison of part-time and full-time employees. *Journal of Occupational Behavior,* in press.

——— (1980). Predicting turnover: An empirical evaluation of the Mobley model and comparison of full-time and part-time employees. Paper presented at the Annual Meeting of the American Psychological Association.

Pettman, D.B. (1973). Some factors influencing labor turnover: A review of the literature. *Industrial Relations Journal* **4**: 43–61.

Porter, L.W., and Lawler, E.E., III (1965). Properties of organizational structure in relation to job attitudes and job behavior. *Psychological Bulletin* **64**: 23–51.

Porter, L.W.; Lawler, E.E.,III; and Hackman, J.R. (1975). *Behavior in Organizations.* New York: McGraw-Hill.

Porter, L.W., and Steers, R.M. (1973). Organizational, work, and personal factors in employee turnover and absenteeism. *Psychological Bulletin* **80**: 151–76.

Porter, L.W.; Steers, R.M.; Mowday, R.T.; and Boulian, P.V. (1974). Organizational commitment, job satisfaction, and turnover among psychiatric technicians. *Journal of Applied Psychology* **59**: 603–9.

Porter, L.W.; Crampon, W.J.; and Smith, F.J. (1976). Organizational commitment and managerial turnover: A longitudinal study. *Organizational Behavior and Human Performance* **15**: 87–98.

Price, J.L. (1975–1976). The measurement of turnover. *Industrial Relations Journal* **6**: 33–46.

——— (1977). *The Study of Turnover.* Ames, Iowa: Iowa State University Press.

Pyle, W.C. (1969). Implementation of human resource accounting in industry. In R.L. Brummet, E.G. Flamholtz, and W.C. Pyle (eds.) *Human Resource Accounting: Development and Implementation in Industry.* Ann Arbor: Foundation for Research on Human Behavior.

Rapoport, R., and Rapoport, R.N. (1976). *Dual Career Families Re-examined.* New York: Harper and Row.

Reid, G.L. (1972). Job search and effectiveness of job finding methods. *Industrial and Labor Relations Review* **25**: 479–95.

Rice, A.K., and Trist, E.L. (1952). Institutional and subinstitutional determinants of change in labor turnover. *Human Relations* **5**: 347–72.

Rizzo, J.R.; House, R.J.; and Lirtzman, S.I. (1970). Role conflict and ambiguity in complex organizations. *Administrative Science Quarterly* **66**: 150–63.

Robinson, W.S. (1950). Ecological correlations and the behavior of individuals. *American Sociological Review* **15**: 351–57.

Ryan, T.A. (1970). *Intentional Behavior: An Approach to Human Motivation.* New York: Ronald Press.

Salancik, G.R.; Staw, B.M.; and Pondy, L.R. (1980). Administrative turnover as a response to unmanaged organizational interdependence. *Academy of Management Journal* **23**: 422–37.

Saleh, S.D.; Lee, R.J.; and Prien, E.P. (1965). Why nurses leave jobs: An analysis of female turnover. *Personnel Administration* **28**: 25–8.

Schein, E.H. (1978). *Career Dynamics: Matching Individual and Organizational Needs.* Reading, Mass.: Addison-Wesley.

Schneider, J. (1976). The "greener grass" phenomenon: Differential effects of a work context alternative on organizational participation and withdrawal intentions. *Organizational Behavior and Human Performance* **16**: 308–33.

Schuler, R.S. (1980). Definition and conceptualization of stress in organizations. *Organizational Behavior and Human Performance* **25**: 184–215.

Schwab, D.P., and Dyer, L.D. (1974). Turnover as a function of perceived ease and desirability: A largely unsuccessful test of the March and Simon participation model. Paper presented at the 34th Annual Meeting of the Academy of Management, Seattle.

Schwab, D.B., and Oliver, R.L. (1974). Predicting tenure with biographical data: Exhuming buried evidence. *Personnel Psychology* **27**: 125–28.

Science Research Associates. (1970). *The SRA Attitude Survey.* Chicago: Science Research Associates, Inc.

Seybolt, J.W.; Pavett, C.; and Walker, D.D. (1978). Turnover among nurses: It can be managed. *Journal of Nursing Administration* **9**: 4–9.

Sharf, J.C. (1979). Uniform guidelines: Competence or numbers. In K.S. McGovern (ed.) *Equal Employment Practice Guide.* Washington: Federal Bar Association, March.

Sheridan, J.E. (1980). A CUSP-catastrophe model of employee turnover. 40th Annual meeting of the Academy of Management, Detroit.

Sheridan, J.E., and Vredenburgh, D.J. (1978). Usefulness of leadership behavior and social power variables in predicting job tension, performance, and turnover of nursing employees. *Journal of Applied Psychology* **63**: 89–95.

Skinner, E. (1969). Relationships between leadership behavior patterns and organizational situational variables. *Personnel Psychology* **22**: 489–94.

Smith, P. (1978). Coming to terms with job crises. *Personnel Management* **10**: 32–5.

Smith, P.C.; Kendall, L.M.; and Hulin, C.L. (1969). *The Measurement of Satisfaction in Work and Retirement.* Chicago: Rand McNally.

Sorenson, J.E.; Rhode, J.G.; and Lawler, E.E., III (1973). The generation gap in public accounting. *Journal of Accounting,* December, 42–50.

Staw, B.M. (1980). The consequences of turnover. *Journal of Occupational Behavior* **1**: 253–73.

Staw, B.M., and Oldham, G.R. (1978). Reconsidering our dependent variables: A critique and empirical study. *Academy of Management Journal* **21**: 539–559.

Steers, R.M. (1977). *Organizational Effectiveness: A Behavioral View.* Santa Monica, Calif.: Goodyear.

Steers, R.M. (1977). Antecedents and outcomes of organizational commitment. *Administrative Science Quarterly* **22**: 46–56.

Steers, R.M., and Mowday, R.T. (1981). Employee turnover and the post decision accommodation process. In B.M. Shaw and L.L. Cummings (eds.) *Research in Organizational Behavior.* Greenwich: JAI Press.

Streyckmans, F.B. (1928). Turning over the turnover problem. *American Gas Journal* March, 34–7.

Tuchi, B.J., and Carr, B.E. (1971). Labor turnover. *Hospitals* **45**: 88–92.

Tuggle, F.D. (1978). An analysis of employee turnover. *Behavioral Science* **23**: 32–7.

U.S. Bureau of Labor Statistics (1980). *Employment and Earnings* 27–4. Washington, D.C.: U.S. Department of Labor.

U.S. Bureau of Labor Statistics (1980). *Monthly Labor Review.* Washington, D.C.: U.S. Department of Labor, 103–4.

U.S. Civil Service Commission (1977). Planning Your Staffing Needs. Washington, D.C.: Bureau of Policies and Standards.

U.S. Department of Defense (1978). *America's Volunteers: A Report on the All-Volunteer Armed Forces,* Washington, D.C.: Office of the Assistant Secretary of Defense, Manpower.

U.S. Department of Labor, OFCCP (1979). *Federal Contract Compliance Manual.* Washington: U.S. Government Printing Office.

U.S. News and World Report (1980). Jobs and family: The walls come down, June 16, 57–8.

Van der Merwe, R., and Miller, S. (1971). The measurement of labor turnover. *Human relations* **24**: 233–53.

——— (1973). Near-terminal labor turnover: An analysis of a crisis situation. *Human Relations* **26**: 415–32.

Van Sell, M.; Brief, A.P.; and Schuler, R.S. (1979). *Role Conflict and Role Ambiguity: Integration of the Literature and Direc-*

tions for Future Research. Working paper. Ames: University of Iowa.

Vickery, C. (1977). The impact of turnover on group unemployment rates. *Review of Economic Statistics* **49**: 415–26.

Vroom, V.H. (1964). *Work and Motivation.* New York: Wiley.

Wachter, M.L. (1980). The labor market mechanism and illegal immigration: The outlook for the 1980's. *Industrial and Labor Relations Review* **33**: 342–54.

Wachter, M.L., and Kim, C. (1979). *Labor Supply: Final Report for ONR.* Philadelphia: Wharton Econometric Forecasting Associates.

Walker, J.W. (1980). *Human Resource Planning.* New York: McGraw-Hill.

Wanous, J.P. (1973). Effects of a realistic job preview on job acceptance, job attitudes, and job survival. *Journal of Applied Psychology* **58**: 327–32.

——— (1980). *Organization Entry: Recruitment, Selection and Socialization of Newcomers.* Reading, Mass.: Addison-Wesley.

Wanous, J.P.; Stumpf, S.A.; and Bedrosian, H. (1979). Job survival of new employees. *Personnel Psychology* **32**: 651–62.

Waters, L.K., and Roach, D. (1973). Job attitudes as predictors of termination and absenteeism: Consistency over time and across organizational units. *Journal of Applied Psychology* **57**: 341–42.

Waters, L.K.; Roach, D.; and Waters, C.W. (1976). Estimate of future tenure, satisfaction, and biographical variables as predictors of termination. *Personnel Psychology* **29**: 57–60.

Weaver, C.N. (1980). Workers expectations about losing and replacing their jobs. *Monthly Labor Review* 103–4, 53–4.

Weiss, D.J.; Dawis, R.V.; England, G.W.; and Lofquist, L.H. (1967). *Manual for the Minnesota Satisfaction Questionnaire.* Minneapolis: University of Minnesota.

Wernick, M.S., and McIntire, J.L. (1980). Employment and labor force growth: Recent trends and future prospects. *Special Study on Economic Change,* Vol. 1, Washington, D.C. U.S.: Government Printing Office, 101–52.

Wertheimer, R.F. (1970). *The Monetary Rewards of Migration within the United States.* Washington, D.C.: The Urban Institute.

Woodman, R.W., and Sherwood, J.J. (1980). The role of team development in organizational effectiveness. *Psychological Bulletin* **88**: 166–86.

Woodward, N. (1975–1976). The economic causes of labor turnover: A case study. *Industrial Relations Journal* **6**: 19–32.

Youngblood, S.A.; Laughlin, J.E.; Mobley, W.H.; and Meglino, B.M. (1980). A longitudinal analysis of military recruit attrition: The first 25 months. *ONR Technical Report,* No. 11, Columbia, S.C.: Center for Management and Organizational Research, University of South Carolina.

Author Index

Subject Index